Carnegie Commission on Higher Education
Sponsored Research Studies

PROFESSIONAL EDUCATION:
SOME NEW DIRECTIONS
Edgar H. Schein

THE NONPROFIT RESEARCH INSTITUTE:
ITS ORIGIN, OPERATION, PROBLEMS, AND
PROSPECTS
Harold Orlans

THE INVISIBLE COLLEGES:
A PROFILE OF SMALL, PRIVATE COLLEGES
WITH LIMITED RESOURCES
Alexander W. Astin and Calvin B. T. Lee

A DEGREE AND WHAT ELSE?:
CORRELATES AND CONSEQUENCES OF A
COLLEGE EDUCATION
*Stephen B. Withey, Jo Anne Coble, Gerald
Gurin, John P. Robinson, Burkhard Strumpel,
Elizabeth Keogh Taylor, and Arthur C. Wolfe*

THE MULTICAMPUS UNIVERSITY:
A STUDY OF ACADEMIC GOVERNANCE
Eugene C. Lee and Frank M. Bowen

INSTITUTIONS IN TRANSITION:
A PROFILE OF CHANGE IN HIGHER
EDUCATION
(INCORPORATING THE 1970 STATISTICAL
REPORT)
Harold L. Hodgkinson

EFFICIENCY IN LIBERAL EDUCATION:
A STUDY OF COMPARATIVE INSTRUCTIONAL
COSTS FOR DIFFERENT WAYS OF ORGANIZ-
ING TEACHING-LEARNING IN A LIBERAL ARTS
COLLEGE
Howard R. Bowen and Gordon K. Douglass

CREDIT FOR COLLEGE:
PUBLIC POLICY FOR STUDENT LOANS
Robert W. Hartman

MODELS AND MAVERICKS:
A PROFILE OF PRIVATE LIBERAL ARTS
COLLEGES
Morris T. Keeton

BETWEEN TWO WORLDS:
A PROFILE OF NEGRO HIGHER EDUCATION
Frank Bowles and Frank A. DeCosta

BREAKING THE ACCESS BARRIERS:
A PROFILE OF TWO-YEAR COLLEGES
Leland L. Medsker and Dale Tillery

ANY PERSON, ANY STUDY:
AN ESSAY ON HIGHER EDUCATION IN THE
UNITED STATES
Eric Ashby

THE NEW DEPRESSION IN HIGHER
EDUCATION:
A STUDY OF FINANCIAL CONDITIONS AT 41
COLLEGES AND UNIVERSITIES
Earl F. Cheit

FINANCING MEDICAL EDUCATION:
AN ANALYSIS OF ALTERNATIVE POLICIES
AND MECHANISMS
Rashi Fein and Gerald I. Weber

HIGHER EDUCATION IN NINE COUNTRIES:
A COMPARATIVE STUDY OF COLLEGES AND
UNIVERSITIES ABROAD
*Barbara B. Burn, Philip G. Altbach, Clark Kerr,
and James A. Perkins*

BRIDGES TO UNDERSTANDING:
INTERNATIONAL PROGRAMS OF AMERICAN
COLLEGES AND UNIVERSITIES
Irwin T. Sanders and Jennifer C. Ward

GRADUATE AND PROFESSIONAL EDUCATION,
1980:
A SURVEY OF INSTITUTIONAL PLANS
Lewis B. Mayhew

THE AMERICAN COLLEGE AND AMERICAN
CULTURE:
SOCIALIZATION AS A FUNCTION OF HIGHER
EDUCATION
Oscar Handlin and Mary F. Handlin

RECENT ALUMNI AND HIGHER EDUCATION:
A SURVEY OF COLLEGE GRADUATES
Joe L. Spaeth and Andrew M. Greeley

CHANGE IN EDUCATIONAL POLICY:
SELF-STUDIES IN SELECTED COLLEGES AND
UNIVERSITIES
Dwight R. Ladd

STATE OFFICIALS AND HIGHER EDUCATION:
A SURVEY OF THE OPINIONS AND
EXPECTATIONS OF POLICY MAKERS IN NINE
STATES
Heinz Eulau and Harold Quinley

ACADEMIC DEGREE STRUCTURES:
INNOVATIVE APPROACHES:
PRINCIPLES OF REFORM IN DEGREE
STRUCTURES IN THE UNITED STATES
Stephen H. Spurr

COLLEGES OF THE FORGOTTEN AMERICANS:
A PROFILE OF STATE COLLEGES AND
REGIONAL UNIVERSITIES
E. Alden Dunham

FROM BACKWATER TO MAINSTREAM:
A PROFILE OF CATHOLIC HIGHER
EDUCATION
Andrew M. Greeley

THE ECONOMICS OF THE MAJOR PRIVATE
UNIVERSITIES
William G. Bowen
*(Out of print, but available from University
Microfilms.)*

THE FINANCE OF HIGHER EDUCATION
Howard R. Bowen
*(Out of print, but available from University
Microfilms.)*

ALTERNATIVE METHODS OF FEDERAL
FUNDING FOR HIGHER EDUCATION
Ron Wolk
*(Out of print, but available from University
Microfilms.)*

INVENTORY OF CURRENT RESEARCH ON
HIGHER EDUCATION 1968
Dale M. Heckman and Warren Bryan Martin
*(Out of print, but available from University
Microfilms.)*

*The following technical reports are available from the Carnegie Commission on Higher Education, 2150
Shattuck Avenue, Berkeley, California 94704.*

RESOURCE USE IN HIGHER EDUCATION:
TRENDS IN OUTPUT AND INPUTS, 1930–1967
June O'Neill

TRENDS AND PROJECTIONS OF PHYSICIANS
IN THE UNITED STATES 1967–2002
Mark S. Blumberg

MAY 1970:
THE CAMPUS AFTERMATH OF CAMBODIA
AND KENT STATE
Richard E. Peterson and John A. Bilorusky

MENTAL ABILITY AND HIGHER EDUCATIONAL
ATTAINMENT IN THE 20TH CENTURY
Paul Taubman and Terence Wales

AMERICAN COLLEGE AND UNIVERSITY
ENROLLMENT TRENDS IN 1971
Richard E. Peterson

PAPERS ON EFFICIENCY IN THE
MANAGEMENT OF HIGHER EDUCATION
*Alexander M. Mood, Colin Bell,
Lawrence Bogard, Helen Brownlee,
and Joseph McCloskey*

AN INVENTORY OF ACADEMIC INNOVATION
AND REFORM
Ann Heiss

ESTIMATING THE RETURNS TO EDUCATION:
A DISAGGREGATED APPROACH
Richard S. Eckaus

SOURCES OF FUNDS TO COLLEGES AND
UNIVERSITIES
June O'Neill

NEW DEPRESSION IN HIGHER
EDUCATION—TWO YEARS LATER
Earl F. Cheit

The following reprints are available from the Carnegie Commission on Higher Education, 2150 Shattuck Avenue, Berkeley, California 94704.

ACCELERATED PROGRAMS OF MEDICAL EDUCATION, by Mark S. Blumberg, reprinted from JOURNAL OF MEDICAL EDUCATION, vol. 46, no. 8, August 1971.*

SCIENTIFIC MANPOWER FOR 1970–1985, by Allan M. Cartter, reprinted from SCIENCE, vol. 172, no. 3979, pp. 132–140, April 9, 1971.

A NEW METHOD OF MEASURING STATES' HIGHER EDUCATION BURDEN, by Neil Timm, reprinted from THE JOURNAL OF HIGHER EDUCATION, vol. 42, no. 1, pp. 27–33, January 1971.*

REGENT WATCHING, by Earl F. Cheit, reprinted from AGB REPORTS, vol. 13, no. 6, pp. 4–13, March 1971.

COLLEGE GENERATIONS—FROM THE 1930s TO THE 1960s by Seymour M. Lipset and Everett C. Ladd, Jr., reprinted from THE PUBLIC INTEREST, no. 25, Summer 1971.

AMERICAN SOCIAL SCIENTISTS AND THE GROWTH OF CAMPUS POLITICAL ACTIVISM IN THE 1960s, by Everett C. Ladd, Jr., and Seymour M. Lipset, reprinted from SOCIAL SCIENCES INFORMATION, vol. 10, no. 2, April 1971.

THE POLITICS OF AMERICAN POLITICAL SCIENTISTS, by Everett C. Ladd, Jr., and Seymour M. Lipset, reprinted from PS, vol. 4, no. 2, Spring 1971.*

THE DIVIDED PROFESSORIATE, by Seymour M. Lipset and Everett C. Ladd, Jr., reprinted from CHANGE, vol. 3, no. 3, pp. 54–60, May 1971.*

JEWISH ACADEMICS IN THE UNITED STATES: THEIR ACHIEVEMENTS, CULTURE AND POLITICS, by Seymour M. Lipset and Everett C. Ladd, Jr., reprinted from AMERICAN JEWISH YEAR BOOK, 1971.

THE UNHOLY ALLIANCE AGAINST THE CAMPUS, by Kenneth Keniston and Michael Lerner, reprinted from NEW YORK TIMES MAGAZINE, November 8, 1970 .

PRECARIOUS PROFESSORS: NEW PATTERNS OF REPRESENTATION, by Joseph W. Garbarino, reprinted from INDUSTRIAL RELATIONS, vol. 10, no. 1, February 1971.*

. . . AND WHAT PROFESSORS THINK: ABOUT STUDENT PROTEST AND MANNERS, MORALS, POLITICS, AND CHAOS ON THE CAMPUS, by Seymour Martin Lipset and Everett C. Ladd, Jr., reprinted from PSYCHOLOGY TODAY, November 1970.*

DEMAND AND SUPPLY IN U.S. HIGHER EDUCATION: A PROGRESS REPORT, by Roy Radner and Leonard S. Miller, reprinted from AMERICAN ECONOMIC REVIEW, May 1970.*

RESOURCES FOR HIGHER EDUCATION: AN ECONOMIST'S VIEW, by Theodore W. Schultz, reprinted from JOURNAL OF POLITICAL ECONOMY, vol. 76, no. 3, University of Chicago, May/ June 1968.*

INDUSTRIAL RELATIONS AND UNIVERSITY RELATIONS, by Clark Kerr, reprinted from PRO-CEEDINGS OF THE 21ST ANNUAL WINTER MEETING OF THE INDUSTRIAL RELATIONS RESEARCH ASSOCIATION, pp. 15–25.*

NEW CHALLENGES TO THE COLLEGE AND UNIVERSITY, by Clark Kerr, reprinted from Kermit Gordon (ed.), AGENDA FOR THE NATION, The Brookings Institution, Washington, D.C., 1968.*

PRESIDENTIAL DISCONTENT, by Clark Kerr, reprinted from David C. Nichols (ed.), PERSPECTIVES ON CAMPUS TENSIONS: PAPERS PREPARED FOR THE SPECIAL COMMITTEE ON CAMPUS TENSIONS, American Council on Education, Washington, D.C., September 1970.*

STUDENT PROTEST—AN INSTITUTIONAL AND NATIONAL PROFILE, by Harold Hodgkinson, reprinted from THE RECORD, vol. 71, no. 4, May 1970.*

WHAT'S BUGGING THE STUDENTS?, by Kenneth Keniston, reprinted from EDUCATIONAL RECORD, American Council on Education, Washington, D.C., Spring 1970.*

THE POLITICS OF ACADEMIA, by Seymour Martin Lipset, reprinted from David C. Nichols (ed.), PERSPECTIVES ON CAMPUS TENSIONS: PAPERS PREPARED FOR THE SPECIAL COMMITTEE ON CAMPUS TENSIONS, American Council on Education, Washington, D.C., September 1970.*

INTERNATIONAL PROGRAMS OF U.S. COLLEGES AND UNIVERSITIES: PRIORITIES FOR THE SEVENTIES, by James A. Perkins, reprinted by permission of the International Council for Educational Development, Occasional Paper no. 1, July 1971.

FACULTY UNIONISM: FROM THEORY TO PRACTICE, by Joseph W. Garbarino, reprinted from INDUSTRIAL RELATIONS, vol. 11, no. 1, pp. 1–17, February 1972.

MORE FOR LESS: HIGHER EDUCATION'S NEW PRIORITY, by Virginia B. Smith, reprinted from UNIVERSAL HIGHER EDUCATION: COSTS AND BENEFITS, American Council on Education, Washington, D.C., 1971.

ACADEMIA AND POLITICS IN AMERICA, by Seymour M. Lipset, reprinted from Thomas J. Nossiter (ed.), IMAGINATION AND PRECISION IN THE SOCIAL SCIENCES, pp. 211–289, Faber and Faber, London, 1972.

POLITICS OF ACADEMIC NATURAL SCIENTISTS AND ENGINEERS, by Everett C. Ladd, Jr., and Seymour M. Lipset, reprinted from SCIENCE, vol. 176, no. 4039, pp. 1091–1100, June 9, 1972.

THE INTELLECTUAL AS CRITIC AND REBEL: WITH SPECIAL REFERENCE TO THE UNITED STATES AND THE SOVIET UNION, by Seymour M. Lipset and Richard B. Dobson, reprinted from DAEDALUS, vol. 101, no. 3, pp. 137–198, Summer 1972.

COMING OF MIDDLE AGE IN HIGHER EDUCATION, by Earl F. Cheit, address delivered to American Association of State Colleges and Universities and National Association of State Universities and Land-Grant Colleges, Washington, D.C., Nov. 13, 1972.

THE NATURE AND ORIGINS OF THE CARNEGIE COMMISSION ON HIGHER EDUCATION, by Alan Pifer, reprinted by permission of The Carnegie Foundation for the Advancement of Teaching, speech delivered to the Pennsylvania Association of Colleges and Universities, Oct. 16, 1972.

THE DISTRIBUTION OF ACADEMIC TENURE IN AMERICAN HIGHER EDUCATION, *by Martin Trow, reprinted from* THE TENURE DEBATE, *Bardwell Smith (ed.), Jossey-Bass, San Francisco, 1972.*

THE POLITICS OF AMERICAN SOCIOLOGISTS, *by Seymour M. Lipset, and Everett C. Ladd, Jr., reprinted from* THE AMERICAN JOURNAL OF SOCIOLOGY, *vol. 78, no. 1, July 1972.*

*The Commission's stock of this reprint has been exhausted.

The Academic
Melting Pot

The Academic Melting Pot

CATHOLICS AND JEWS
IN AMERICAN HIGHER EDUCATION

by **Stephen Steinberg**

*Graduate School and University Center,
The City University of New York*

A Report Prepared for
The Carnegie Commission on Higher Education

MCGRAW-HILL BOOK COMPANY
New York   St. Louis   San Francisco   Düsseldorf
London   Sydney   Toronto   Mexico   Panama
Johannesburg   Kuala Lumpur   Montreal
New Delhi   São Paulo   Singapore

*The Carnegie Commission on Higher Education,
2150 Shattuck Avenue, Berkeley, California 94704,
has sponsored preparation of this volume as a
part of a continuing effort to obtain and present
significant information for public discussion.
The views expressed are those of the author.*

THE ACADEMIC MELTING POT
Catholics and Jews in American Higher Education

Library of Congress Cataloging in Publication Data

Steinberg, Stephen.
The academic melting pot.
Originally presented as the author's thesis,
University of California, Berkeley.
1. Education, Higher—United States. 2. Catholics
in the United States—Intellectual life. 3. Jews in
the United States—Intellectual life. I. Carnegie
Commission on Higher Education. II. Title.
III. Title: Catholics and Jews in American higher
education.
LA226.S69 1973   378.73   73-9656
ISBN 0-07-010067-5

123456789MAMM7987654

To my parents

Contents

List of Tables

Foreword

In America, the notions of Jewish "intellectualism" and Catholic "anti-intellectualism" have existed since the first great waves of immigrants entered the American public schools—institutions that were Protestant-influenced and strongly committed to the acculturation of foreigners. Many Jewish immigrants came to this country with a high literacy rate and experience in industrial work and consequently felt more comfortable with the values of the existing public school system. They enrolled in this system and eventually began to compete academically with the Protestant upper-middle-class in colleges and universities. Most Catholic immigrants, on the other hand, had a relatively low literacy rate and came from a peasant background. Both these factors impeded their class mobility and handicapped the performance of Catholic children in school. For these, and for religious reasons, Catholics tended to reject secular schools in favor of their own. The consequences of the different courses taken by these two immigrant groups are evident today in higher education: Jews are proportionately over-represented on the faculty of ranking universities and produce a large amount of scholarly research, whereas Catholics have been underrepresented and less productive in research.

Stephen Steinberg thoroughly analyzes Catholic-Jewish attitudes toward education, using both a historical method—beginning with Jews in the shtetls of Eastern Europe and Catholic tenant farmers in Southern Italy—and an examination of data from the 1969 Carnegie Commission Survey on Faculty and Student Opinion.

Data from the 1969 survey supports the historical view that the American education system functions as a melting pot. Catholics are now becoming proportionately represented, and even over-represented, in the undergraduate populations of universities and colleges, though an educational philosophy born of a Catholic background may still be reflected in many ways—in a commitment to teaching rather than to research or in a tendency to study the humanities rather than the more applied scientifically based disciplines. The original Protestant and elitist character of higher education has clearly changed and the "Jewish influx" is leveling off.

Out of the survey data come many other interesting findings, including those hinging on the relationships of scholarship and academic success to religious belief and degree of religiosity and those that relate religion and scholarship to political beliefs. Professor Steinberg discusses these and other findings in detail.

Several forthcoming Carnegie Commission publications will examine other aspects of this data—notably the study of the politics of American academics by Everett C. Ladd, Jr. and Seymour Martin Lipset, Saul Feldman's *Escape from the Doll's House: Women in Graduate and Professional School Education,* and a collection of essays edited by Martin Trow. As the first of these publications, Professor Steinberg's study makes a significant contribution to our understanding of the complex forces that have molded American higher education.

Clark Kerr

Chairman
The Carnegie Commission
on Higher Education

May 1973

Acknowledgments

This study is based in part on data collected by the National Surveys of Higher Education, sponsored by the Carnegie Commission on Higher Education and supported in part as a cooperative research project by funds from the United States Office of Education. I am grateful to these agencies for their financial assistance.

The surveys on which the data analysis is based were monumental undertakings. Separate surveys were conducted of faculty, graduate students, and undergraduates in hundreds of institutions of higher learning throughout the United States. Major credit belongs to Martin Trow, the project director, whose experience and research skill were invaluable to the success of the project.

When I joined the project's staff in 1970, all the field work and data processing had been completed. I therefore am indebted to the individuals responsible for planning and implementing these surveys. In addition to Martin Trow they are: Ted Bradshaw, Saul Feldman, Oliver Fulton, Travis Hirschi, Carlos Kruytbosch, Judy Roizen, and Joseph Zelan. To the able and spirited staff at the Survey Research Center, I owe thanks not only for their considerable assistance, but also for their creation of such a congenial setting in which to work.

This book was originally written as a Ph.D. dissertation at the University of California, Berkeley, under the supervision of Charles Glock, Robert Blauner, and Martin Trow. They stood for standards of excellence, but at the same time gave me the freedom to pursue my own instincts, especially when I ventured into the domain of history. Faruk Birtek, Forest Dill, and Calvin Goldscheider read portions of the manuscript and made helpful comments. Judith Steinberg was my most valuable source of feedback. She was a good listener and a persistent critic and, between chapters, a tireless traveling companion.

During my graduate years at Berkeley I had the opportunity to work closely with Charles Glock and Gertrude Selznick. They were both mentors and friends, and in one way or another their influence permeates this book. I am happy to acknowledge my personal debt to each of them.

The Academic
Melting Pot

Part One

Immigrants and American Educational Institutions

Until the beginning of the twentieth century American higher education had an unmistakably Protestant cast. Most of the leading colleges had been founded by religious denominations, often with the specific purpose of training missionaries and producing an educated ministry. The intellectual and moral climate was heavily tinged with Calvinism, and the main purpose of a college education was understood to be the cultivation of mental and moral discipline. Compulsory prayers and church services occupied no small portion of a student's daily regimen, and religious revivals were commonplace. The vast majority of faculty and students also were Protestant.

The influx of millions of Catholic and Jewish immigrants during the great migrations of the nineteenth and early twentieth centuries drastically altered the religious composition of the nation, and in doing so, set the stage for the ultimate de-Protestantization of higher education. Over time, American colleges and universities would become less exclusively Protestant, not only in numbers but in character and outlook as well.

The educational history of Catholics and Jews in America is one of striking contrasts. The waves of Catholic immigration preceded or coincided with Jewish immigration, yet Catholics did not make significant inroads into American higher education until much later. Jewish immigrants carried with them an intellectual tradition that, despite its antiquated religious framework, facilitated the adjustment to secular education in America. At a time when Jewish immigrants were eagerly sending their children off to college, Catholic leaders were issuing dire warnings concerning the dangers of secular schools. Even when threatened with restrictive quotas, Jews rejected the idea of building their own colleges.[1] Catholics, on the other hand, chose to develop an elaborate system of parish schools and Catholic colleges. Finally, Jews have produced a disproportionate number of scholars and scientists, whereas Catholics historically have been underrepresented in these spheres.

If Jews and Catholics approached secular education with different sentiments, the response of the Protestant majority was also different in each case. The fact that Jews entered institutions of higher learning before they were fully acculturated helped to trigger a xenophobic reaction, especially in the elite Eastern colleges. By the time that Catholics entered American colleges in large numbers, they were fairly well assimilated and the era of intense anti-Catholic prejudice had subsided. Instead it was the lower schools that served as the battleground for a prolonged and acrimonious conflict between Catholics and the Protestant majority.

Part I of this study deals with the disparate experiences of Jewish and Catholic immigrants as they encountered American educational institutions. No attempt is made to write a complete history of this encounter. Rather, two critical moments in the educational history of Jews and Catholics are examined in detail.

The first chapter deals with an episode that occurred at Harvard College in 1922. In that year President Lowell indiscreetly announced that a plan was under consideration to limit the college's Jewish enrollment, which had increased to nearly 20 percent. While other of the Eastern elite colleges had already taken similar action to deal with their "Jewish problem," Harvard was the first to publicly defend religious restrictions, and in doing so, brought the issue to the surface for the first time. While the chapter focuses on the Harvard affair, which has received only scant attention in previous research, its broader purpose is to analyze the factors that

---

[1] For example, a 1922 editorial in the *American Hebrew* commented: "The recent proposal to establish a Jewish University in the United States bespeaks a lamentable lack of confidence in the justice and fair play of the American people. . . . Segregation of Jewish students would sound the knell of Jewish equality in the political as well as the intellectual life of this country." With reference to Catholic schools, the editorial declared: "While we have only the highest respect for our neighbors' religion, we nevertheless do not see the necessity of following their example. We do not need to protect our coreligionists from the inroads of other creeds in that manner. A faith that has stood unshaken for thousands of years does not require cloistered walls or academic seclusion to retain its integrity. The proposal is altogether ill-advised and not in any sense representative of the wishes of American Jewry" ("Why a Jewish University?" 1922, p. 35).

both facilitated and obstructed Jewish entry into American higher education.

There was no comparable Catholic "invasion" of American colleges. Rather, the educational thrust within the Catholic community was in the direction of separatism. The purpose of Chapter 2 is to analyze the factors that led Catholics to establish their own system of education, a movement that began around the middle of the nineteenth century and established its basic character by the end of the century. Needless to say, a single chapter cannot provide a comprehensive account of a movement that spanned a century. Rather, its purpose is to analyze the sources of Catholic hostility toward public education, a subject around which there has been much serious misunderstanding.

Together these chapters will provide a historical context for the data analysis of later chapters.

1. The "Jewish Problem" in Higher Education

In his well-known history of *Three Centuries of Harvard,* Samuel Eliot Morison had this to say of Harvard's Jewish studies: "The first German Jews who came were easily absorbed into the social pattern; but at the turn of the century the bright Russian Jewish lads from the Boston public schools began to arrive. There were enough of them in 1906 to form the Menorah Society, and *in another fifteen years Harvard had her 'Jewish problem'"* (Morison, 1936, p. 147, italics added).[1] What does it mean to have a "Jewish problem"? From the vantage point of Abbott Lawrence Lowell, president of Harvard from 1909 to 1933, the problem was that the increasing numbers of Jewish students at Harvard threatened to alter the traditional character of the college. To the Jews of the period, if there was a "Jewish problem" at Harvard, it was that the university for the first time was preparing to impose religious quotas.

By 1922 Columbia and New York University had already taken steps to restrict their Jewish enrollment. But they had done so covertly, relying on character tests and regional quotas to conceal their intentions. Harvard was different only in being the first to openly advocate and defend a quota system. In June 1922, the university issued an official announcement that began by taking note of a recent increase in student enrollment and a shortage of classrooms and dormitories. The announcement then moved to some oblique but ominous language: "This problem is really a group of problems, all difficult, and most of them needing for their settlement more facts than we now have." And finally: "It is natural that with a widespread discussion of this sort going on there should be talk about the proportion of Jews at the college. At present the

[1] Copyright © 1936 by the President and Fellows of Harvard College. Reprinted by permission of Harvard University Press.

5

whole problem of limitation of enrollment is in the stage of general discussion and it may remain in that stage for a considerable time" (*New York Times,* June 2, 1922, p. 1).

This event at Harvard culminated a 40-year period of evolving confrontation between American Jews and the system of higher education. It was an outgrowth of a large number of historical trends: patterns of immigration around the turn of the century, the Jewish "invasion" of institutions of higher learning, the rise of virulent anti-Semitism in the society, the transformation of higher education from classical traditions to scientific education and vocational training, and the decline of certain status groups whose prerogatives were being challenged by a rising bourgeoisie. Some of these trends involved Jews directly; others did so only incidentally. Some were conducive to Jewish aspirations; other posed obstacles. In either case, the Jewish experience in higher education was a part of much larger social trends, and the "Jewish problem" at Harvard was a manifestation, though a special one, of the "Jewish problem" in early twentieth-century America.

THE EMERGENCE OF A "JEWISH PROBLEM"

We can accept Morison's contention that the arrival of Russian and Polish Jews at Harvard marked the beginning of its "Jewish problem." Generally speaking, this was true for the country as a whole. Prior to the influx of East European Jews beginning in 1881, the nation's Jewish population was a small, inconspicuous, and highly assimilated group. Most were either descendents of early settlers or recent German immigrants. In all they numbered roughly a quarter of a million in a population of 63 million, or just six-tenths of one percent. As Nathan Glazer (1955, p. 9) comments, ". . . before 1880 or 1890 there were too few American Jews for them to constitute a question."

More than small numbers was involved. Given their German origins, Jews blended in culturally with the American mainstream. By 1880 the great majority had entered middle-class occupations. The prevailing mood in the Jewish community was to abandon outmoded beliefs and customs and to seek ways to reconcile historical Judaism with the demands of modern society. This was the period during which the Reform Movement flourished and reached its most radical expression. In 1885 a group of leading Reform rabbis adopted a statement of principles that rejected whatever in Mosaic legislation was "not adapted to the views and habits of modern civilization" (Glazer, 1957, p. 151).

With reference to the early nineteenth century, one historian writes: "A negligible factor in point of numbers, the [Jews] were not the object of any confederated denunciations and any vestige of even a tentative movement against them was absent" (Myers, 1960, p. 71). Another historian observes that despite many incidents of anti-Semitism, "the prevailing temper of the 19th century [for Jews] was overwhelmingly tolerant" (Handlin, 1951, p. 541). However, another historian of the period was more skeptical: ". . . the Jews in early nineteenth century America got along very well with their non-Jewish neighbors *although American conceptions of Jews in the abstract at no time lacked the unfavorable elements embedded in European traditions.*"[2]

This qualification is crucial to an understanding of the period after 1880. It would be more accurate to characterize the nineteenth century in terms of a relative absence of overt hostility and discrimination, rather than as an era of tolerance. The presence of anti-Semitic conceptions, however inert, did not augur well for the immigrants from Eastern Europe who began coming en masse after 1880. Even before their arrival, upwardly mobile Jews with German origins confronted social barriers erected by a nervous Protestant upper class. The economic expansion after mid-century created a new class of wealthy capitalists, some Jews among them, who challenged the position of the "Old Guard." It was largely in response to this development that "after 1880 the longings for exclusive, quasi-aristocratic status increasingly found satisfaction in associations with an hereditary basis" (Handlin, 1955). Yankee ancestry became a condition for respectability, and the old class sought refuge in exclusive societies and resorts. According to one writer: "During the 1880s anti-Semitic discriminations spread like wildfire through the vacation grounds of New York State and the Jersey shore" (Higham, 1957, p. 12). Discrimination also became the practice in prestigious clubs, including some university alumni clubs, and in certain private schools in the East.

Although anti-Semitism had its foundations prior to the East European immigration, before this period anti-Semitism did not assume the dimensions of a "Jewish problem." Anti-Semitic imagery existed but there were simply too few Jews—especially lower-class and ethnically different Jews—for the stereotypes to be salient

---

[2] Higham (1957, p. 3, italics added). Higham's excellent bibliography brought my attention to some of the important resource material used in this chapter.

even to Americans with nativist tendencies. The key to understanding the transformation that occurred is found in the magnitude and nature of the Jewish immigration from Eastern Europe.

In 1880 the Jewish population of the United States was only 250,000, or less than 1 percent of the population. By 1924, the year that immigration quotas were imposed, the nation's Jewish population had grown to nearly 4 million. Moreover, Jews were heavily concentrated in the urban centers of the Northeast, where they did in fact constitute a significant portion of the population. The Jewish population of New York, the port of arrival for most immigrants, grew from 80,000 in 1880 to 1,225,000 in 1910 (Glazer & Moynihan, 1963). From a practically invisible minority of 3 percent, Jews grew to 30 percent of the city's population in 1920. To native New Yorkers of the period, the idea of a "Jewish invasion" was more than nativist fantasy.

Even more important than the increase in numbers was the social character of the newer immigrants. Impoverished, refugees from persecution, natives of an alien and sometimes backward culture, adherents of pre-modern religious beliefs and customs, the East European Jews were a new and visible factor in American life. The spectacle of over 1 million Jews clustered in New York City aroused the predictable xenophobic reaction. America now had a "Jewish problem," and American nativism a new target.

The essence of the "Jewish problem" was how to control the influx of Jews into areas of social activity that were predominantly Protestant. By 1920 a pattern of anti-Jewish discrimination had become established, especially in the Northeast, where the Jewish settlements were located. Discrimination became commonplace in neighborhoods, clubs, resorts, and private boarding schools, and was making headway wherever else Jews turned in large numbers.

For Jews the pervasiveness of social discrimination reinforced a tendency to withdraw into their own communities and to establish their own institutions. This mood was reflected in the Reform Movement, which lost much of its earlier idealism and militancy (Steinberg, 1965). Traditions were reinstituted that only a few years before had been rejected as unenlightened, and the movement no longer held the reconciliation of Judaism to the demands of modern society as a primary objective. The immediate prospects were not for equal participation in democratic society but for a collective assault on discriminatory institutions. The spirit of Reform was replaced by the self-protective concerns embodied in the Jewish defense agencies founded during this period.[3]

Perhaps the most important thing to be said about the period between 1910 and 1920 is that a climate of intolerance toward Jews had developed in the nation. Manifested in patterns of social discrimination and sustained by an upsurge in anti-Semitic propaganda, anti-Semitism now figured prominently in American life. Jews, whether German or Russian, middle-class or lower-class, were lumped together with other aliens who were threatening Anglo-Saxon supremacy. The Eastern colleges—elitist, tradition-bound repositories of Puritan values and upper-class standards—could not remain untouched by these trends, especially when their enrollments contained increasing numbers of Jewish students.

THE JEWISH PENCHANT FOR EDUCATION

"The Jew undergoes privation, spills blood, to educate his child," boasts an editorial in a 1902 *Jewish Daily Forward* (Sanders, 1969, pp. 259–260). "In [this] is reflected one of the finest qualities of the Jewish people. It shows our capacity to make sacrifices for our children . . . as well as our love for education, for intellectual effort." While the Jewish passion for education is often romanticized, the fact is that Jewish immigrants did place high value on education and sent their children to college in disproportionate numbers. As the *Forward*'s editorial observed: "You don't find many German, Irish or Italian children in City College. About 90 percent of the boys there are Jews, and most of them children of Jewish workers." What the *Forward* neglected to mention was that, according to one early report, "as the percentage of Russian-Jewish boys in attendance increased, the families of Anglo-Saxon, Dutch, German, and Huguenot descent, who had been accustomed to register their boys in the College in the old days, sent them elsewhere for a college education" (Rudy, 1949, pp. 292–293).

As more and more Jews enrolled in City College, it acquired a reputation for being a "Jewish school." Indeed, by 1920 both City College and Hunter College had become between 80 and 90 percent Jewish. A number of other Eastern colleges showed rapid increases in their Jewish enrollment (Broun & Britt, 1931, pp. 104–123). Before Columbia instituted restrictive quotas after World War I, it had a Jewish enrollment of 40 percent. The figure for New York University was probably higher; the figure for Harvard was 20 percent. Without its pejorative implications, the notion of a "Jewish inva-

---

[3] The American Jewish Committee was founded in 1906; the Anti-Defamation League in 1913.

sion" would not be inappropriate for describing the trends in these institutions prior to World War I.

The high rate of college attendance among Jews is easier to understand against the background of conditions in the secondary schools. During the early 1900s American society did not place much value on a continuing education. The vast majority of Americans were employed in occupations that required few skills, especially of a kind that comes with formal education. For most people anything beyond a rudimentary knowledge of the three R's had little practical value, and the tendency in the schools was to emphasize "life adjustment" rather than intellectual development with an eye to college preparation. The individual who graduated from high school was the exception, not the rule. Those who did complete high school came mostly from the economically advantaged strata of society. They alone could afford to postpone employment and could see in a high school or college education some prospective utility and economic benefit.

Nevertheless, the common school did provide an opportunity for those in the lower classes with sufficient ingenuity or will to obtain free education for their children. Jews availed themselves of this opportunity with greater frequency than most other groups. A 1922 study of one Eastern high school found that the academic record of Russian Jewish students was surpassed only by children of German or Scandinavian parents. In comparison to most other immigrant groups, as well as to native Americans, Jewish children were more likely to reach high school, more likely to finish high school if they entered, and more likely to enroll in college preparatory rather than commercial or scientific courses.[4]

From a historical perspective it makes little sense to explain Jewish academic success in terms of a special aptitude or native genius on the part of Jews.[5] It was enough that Jews placed high value on

[4] Counts (1922, p. 108). The study was conducted in Bridgeport, Connecticut. The author found similar results in Mt. Vernon, New York. Another study in the 1920s showed that Jews constituted 30 percent of the enrollment of New York's elementary schools but 55 percent of the high school enrollment (Broun & Britt, 1931, p. 72).

[5] Biological theories that purport to explain Jewish prominence among intellectuals as an expression of genetic factors have more than popular currency; they have also been proposed by serious writers. See Wiener (1966, pp. 11–12); van den Haag (1969, Ch. 1); and Weyl (1966). The present study in its totality argues against these intellectually regressive theories.

education, that they were more often willing to undergo sacrifices, and that their children had the motivation and perseverance to stay in school when most of their contemporaries had liberated themselves from academic routine and discipline.

Nor did it demand any special talent to gain admission to college, even a prestigious college. Fifty years ago the gates to most of the nation's colleges were open to anyone with only minimal academic credentials. In 1922 admission to Harvard was guaranteed to high school graduates who passed an entrance examination. The fact of the matter is that Jews did not face intense competition from non-Jews, at least not on the scale that is characteristic today. With determination, average intellect, and modest financial resources, a student could make his way through the academic system.[6]

The fact that the Jewish assault on institutions of higher learning began with second- rather than third- or fourth-generation Jews was of utmost significance. Jewish college students during the 1920s carried the mark of their immigrant backgrounds. A writer in a 1923 edition of the *Nation* put it bluntly: the upwardly mobile Jew "sends his children to college a generation or two sooner than other stocks, and as a result there are in fact more dirty Jews and tactless Jews in college than dirty and tactless Italians, Armenians, or Slovaks" (Gannett, 1923, p. 331). The editorial in the *Jewish Daily Forward* could take pride in Jewish students marching off to City College with clothes that were "mostly poor and old." But they were greeted with indignation and hostility by their upper-class schoolmates, especially in the elite Eastern colleges.

THE TRANS-FORMATION OF HIGHER EDUCATION   No matter how strong the Jewish penchant for education, no matter how deeply it was rooted in Jewish religion and culture, it would have mattered for little if room had not existed in the colleges. It was fortuitous that the tide of Jewish immigration from Eastern Europe coincided with a period of unprecedented expansion in American higher education. Between 1890 and 1925 college enrollments grew nearly five times faster than the population (Rudolph, 1962, p. 442).

---

[6] Nor were the costs of education as much an obstacle as they are today. At Harvard, for example, "in 1887 nearly as many men spent between $450 and $650 a year as ran through amounts above $1,200 in the same time. One man spent $400, another $4,000" (Veysey, 1965, p. 289). Public institutions, such as City College, were tuition-free.

Just as important as the physical expansion of the university were the related qualitative changes. For several decades a revolt had been gaining momentum against a curriculum that consisted principally of Latin, Greek, rhetoric, mathematics, and natural philosophy. By 1880 the attitude that all knowledge must begin with the classics gave way to demands for practical education. "Vocational and technical education had become a legitimate function of American higher education, and everywhere the idea of going to college was being liberated from the class-bound, classical-bound traditions which for so long had defined the American college experience" (ibid., p. 263). Behind this changing conception of higher education was the advancing industrial and scientific revolution that created a need for an educated managerial class as well as for trained professionals and technicians.

By abandoning its lofty pretensions, the American college became compatible with the abilities and aspirations of those born outside the upper classes. It did so in several ways. Latin and Greek were no longer required for admission to most colleges, and the "elective principle" was instituted to free students from traditionally required subjects. It was generally conceded that training students for careers in business, engineering, scientific farming and the arts was compatible with the ideals of a college, and a variety of new professions, such as accounting and pharmacy, made their appearance in American colleges for the first time. Thanks to their penchant for education and their determination to succeed, Jews availed themselves of the newly created opportunities more than did other groups. Thanks to the basic structural changes in society that transformed American higher education, the opportunities existed in the first place.

THE GENTEEL TRADITION There are always incongruities in the wake of rapid change, and some of those produced by the academic reforms discussed above had direct bearing on the "Jewish problem." A large number of new colleges, many under public control, were founded after 1880, and never experienced a conflict between the old and the new. Others, including Yale and Princeton, resisted the new trends and thereby avoided discord for a time. Still others, notably Harvard and Columbia, were caught in the ebb of change. By introducing curricular reform and opening their doors to persons without upper-class credentials, they became the battlegrounds for a struggle between the old class and the rising bourgeoisie.

One writer in 1910 observed that in American colleges there were "two classes, the one, favored according to undergraduate thinking, holding its position by financial ability to have a good time with leisure for carrying off athletic and other showy prizes; the other class in sheer desperation taking the faculty, textbooks and debating more seriously. Each class runs in the same rut all its life" (Veysey, 1965, pp. 270–271). Second-generation Jews obviously did not have the economic resources or the social standing to participate in the collegiate "leisure class." For them a college education was less a mark of status than a vehicle out of the lower class, and this inevitably gave Jews a sense of purpose lacking among children from privileged backgrounds.

Numerous writers during the early 1900s commented on the outstanding academic record of Jewish students. According to a report of the Industrial Commission: "In the lower schools the Jewish children are the delight of their teachers for cleverness at their books, obedience, and general good conduct" (Glazer, 1955, p. 14). Another writer comments: "At every university and college that I have visited, I have heard ungrudging praise of the exceptional ability of the Jewish, especially of the Russian Jewish, students" (Francis, 1909, p. 187). Even those uneasy about the influx of Jews rarely denied their enterprise as students. One comments begrudgingly: "History is full of examples where one race has displaced another by underliving and overworking" (Cook, 1927, p. 125). Indeed, Jewish academic success and the willingness of Jews to violate the "taboo on scholarship" (as one Yale professor called it) were sources of considerable resentment, and constituted no small part of the "Jewish problem."

Nothing more need be said about the class of students who took faculty, textbooks, and debating seriously; they were not very different from the contemporary college student with serious aspirations, a competitive spirit, and a respect for scholarship. The really significant thing about Jews is that they possessed these qualities long before they became established as norms in the better universities. Early in the century, the prevailing mood in the American college, especially the prestigious Eastern colleges, was anything but one of seriousness and devotion to learning. According to one historian: "The undergraduate temperament was marked by a strong resistance to abstract thinking and to the work of the classroom in general, by traits of practicality, romanticism, and high-spiritedness, and by passive acceptance of moral, political, and religious values taken from the nonacademic society at large" (Veysey, 1965, p. 272).[7]

Another historian of the period writes:

Now what mattered for so many young men was not the course of study but the environment of friendships, social development, fraternity houses, good sportsmanship, athletic teams. The world of business was a world of dealing with people. What better preparation could there be than the collegiate life outside the classroom—the club room, the playing field, where the qualities that showed what stuff a fellow really was made of were bound to be encouraged (Rudolph, 1962, p. 289).[8]

It would be difficult to exaggerate the extent to which honor societies, Greek-letter fraternities, eating clubs, and sports dominated undergraduate life. "The cultivation of gentility," as Thorstein Veblen called it, was pursued to the exclusion of virtually all other values. The prevailing attitude toward scholarship was at best one of indifference, as symbolized by the concept and reality of the "gentleman's C."

The class origins of students in the elite colleges were of central importance. Recruited largely from upper-class families, their route to college typically traversed the private preparatory school where they were initiated into a career in gentility. In 1909, for example, 78 percent of Princeton students and 65 percent of Yale students came from prep schools (ibid.). Significantly, the figure for Harvard was lower—47 percent. In these colleges, upper-class students established a clubbish atmosphere and patterns of expensive and frivolous habits. Veblen bluntly called them "gentlemen's colleges" where "scholarship is . . . made subordinate to genteel dissipation, to a grounding in those methods of conspicuous consumption that should engage the thought and energies of a well-to-do man of the world" (Veblen, 1957, pp. 87–88)

It was no doubt reflective of class formations elsewhere in society that higher education assumed the features of a caste system. At the top of the hierarchy stood Harvard, Yale, and Princeton, with Columbia struggling to retain its elite position. Within each institution was a wealthy class who dominated social life and set patterns imitated throughout the system of higher education. The leading institutions were measured more in terms of these status character-

---

[7] From *The Emergence of the American University*. Copyright © 1965 by the University of Chicago. All rights reserved. Published 1965. Reprinted by permission of the publisher.

[8] From *The American College and University*. Copyright © 1962 by Frederick Rudolph. Published by Random House, Inc. Reprinted by permission.

istics than by standards of scholarship or academic achievement.

The important thing to be said about Jews is that they threatened this respectability. They did so, first of all, because they were lower-class, and frequently exhibited ethnic characteristics that violated what Veblen called "the canons of genteel intercourse." Secondly, the seriousness and diligence with which they pursued their studies not only represented unwelcome competition, but implicitly called into question the propriety of a "gentlemen's college." Finally, Jews were unwanted simply because they were Jews, and it was feared that their presence might diminish the social standing of the college and its students.

Some of the flavor of this conflict is conveyed in an autobiographical essay entitled "The Coming of the Jews." The author, Francis Russell, came from an old-guard Protestant family. After a few years at Roxbury Latin, a fashionable private school, he switched to Boston Latin School, an elite public high school that sent its best students to Harvard. By 1920 it had become heavily Jewish. With a mixture of admiration and scorn, Russell contrasts his own middle-class assumptions with the drive and competitiveness of his Jewish classmates:

My own background was middle-class, Protestant, noncompetitive, like that of most Roxbury Latin boys. I had always taken for granted that I should go to Harvard because my father in his time had gone there; and I never doubted the possibility of this any more than I stopped to consider whether I really wanted to or not. That Harvard could be the goal of anyone's ambitions never occurred to me (Russell, 1955, p. 32).

In contrast,

[Jews] worked far into each night, their lessons next morning were letter perfect, they took obvious pride in their academic success and talked about it. At the end of each year there were room prizes given for excellency in each subject, and they were openly after them. There was none of the Roxbury solidarity of pupils versus the master. If anyone reciting made a mistake that the master overlooked, twenty hands shot into the air to bring it to his attention (ibid., p. 33).[9]

Such a competitive situation does not generate good feeling, especially when the group with superior status takes second place. As Russell says: "It was a fierce and gruelling competition. . . . Some of us in the Gentile rump were fair students, most of us lazy and

mediocre ones, and by our position at the foot of the class we de-
spised the industry of those little Jews." It was just as inevitable
that Jews would begrudge the status and privilege of their competi-
tors: "They hated us in return with the accumulated resentment of
the past, and because they knew that the way for us was easier"
(ibid., p. 34).[10]

The picture that emerges from Russell's candid essay is of a com-
placent ruling class living off past achievements, suddenly challenged by a class of talented upstarts who are resented all the more
because they are Jewish. For the first time the conflict between the
status interests and the educational functions of the elite colleges re-
vealed itself. As a 1922 journal put it: "Each student in an American college is there, or is supposed to be there, for some other purpose than acquiring knowledge. He is to be the transmitter to others
of ideals of mind, spirit, and conduct. *Scholarship is perhaps the
most strongly emphasized of these ideals, but it is not the only one,
or even the one most generally prized"* ("Exclusion from College,"
1922, p. 406, italics added). No one suggested that Jewish students
threatened academic standards. Rather they contended that the college stood for *other* things, and that social standards were as important and valid as intellectual ones.

RAISING THE BARRIERS A college song during the 1910s had these lyrics:

Oh, Harvard's run by millionaires,
And Yale is run by booze,
Cornell is run by farmers' sons
Columbia's run by Jews.

---

[10] The view from the other side is suggested by the following passage from Norman Podhoretz's autobiography, *Making It*. Podhoretz is describing his high
school teacher, a New England patrician, who took it upon herself to tutor him
in manners: "To her the most offensive of the [uncouth] ways was the style in
which I dressed: a tee shirt, tightly pegged pants, and a red satin jacket with the
legend 'Cherokees, S.A.C.' (social-athletic club) stitched in large white letters
across the back. This was bad enough, but when on certain days I would appear
in school wearing, as a particular ceremonial occasion required, a suit and tie,
the sight of those immense padded shoulders and my white-on-white shirt
would drive her to even greater heights of loving despair than usual. *Slum child,
filthy little slum child.* I was beyond saving; I deserved no better than to wind up
with all the other horrible little Jewboys in the gutter (by which she meant
Brooklyn College). If only I would listen to her the whole world could be mine:
I could win a scholarship to Harvard, I could get to know the best people, I could
grow up into a life of elegance and refinement and taste" (p. 10, italics in original). Copyright © 1967 by Norman Podhoretz. Published by Random House,
Inc. Reprinted by permission.

So give a cheer for Baxter Street,
Another one for Pell
And when the little sheenies die,
Their souls will go to hell.

A climate of intolerance prevailed in many Eastern colleges long before discriminatory quotas were contemplated by college officials. From the turn of the century anti-Semitism was a common feature of campus social life. Although exceptions were sometimes made, Jews were generally excluded from the honor societies and eating clubs at Yale and Princeton (Hapgood, 1916a, p. 54). In 1902 a dormitory at Harvard came to be known as "Little Jerusalem" because of its large number of Jewish residents (Earnest, 1953, p. 216). In 1913 a fraternity suspended its charter at CCNY because "the Hebraic element is greatly in excess" (Rudy, 1949, p. 294). Such anti-Semitic incidents checker the history of American colleges after 1900. A 1930 survey under Jewish sponsorship summed things up this way: "Manifestations of anti-Jewish feeling took the following forms: slurring remarks, social aloofness, exclusion from honorary fraternities . . . discrimination in campus politics . . . offensive jokes in student publications and student dramatics, general unfriendliness" (Broun & Britt, 1931, p. 91).

However unpleasant, social discrimination was not a serious disability. For one thing, Jews tended to avoid such campuses as Yale and Princeton which had a reputation for bigotry, and to seek out others—City College, New York University, and Columbia—that offered a less hostile atmosphere as well as proximity to New York's Lower East Side. Under President Eliot's administration, Harvard earned a reputation as the most liberal and democratic of the "Big Three" and therefore Jews did not feel that the avenue to a prestigious college was altogether closed (Veysey, 1965, pp. 288–289; Hapgood, 1916a, p. 54). Although campus anti-Semitism probably left Jews with a feeling of social inferiority, it was a small price to pay for education and economic advancement. The author of a 1916 article in *Harper's Weekly* went so far as to see social discrimination as an asset: ". . . indeed, their exclusion from societies stimulates their education on the intellectual side; and a final judgement on the whole matter would depend in part on the relative importance we give to 'college work' and 'college life' " (Hapgood, 1916b, p. 78). His prediction that Jews would pioneer a "new and higher conception of the purpose of university education" may have proved correct in some respects. But the immediate result of Jewish exclusion often was that Jews formed their own fraternities and social groups. Ironically, this only reinforced the prevalent notion that Jewish students were clannish and unassimilable.

At least some administrators of Eastern colleges shared the anti-Jewish sentiments of their students, hardly surprising since both groups had similar social origins. In 1890 the editor of the *American Hebrew* mailed a questionnaire to a number of prominent Christians, including several college presidents and professors (Cowen, 1928). Those who replied were unanimous in condemning prejudice as indefensible and irrational, but a question concerning "standards of conduct" elicited some critical comments about Jews. The president of the University of Vermont wrote:

> Wherever . . . Jews have . . . fallen in with the social customs of the community, they have . . . been received and treated like other Americans. Whereas in certain summer resorts within my observation—they have kept themselves together, and apart from others, and massed themselves on the piazza, and in the drawing rooms, and at the tables, they have been objected to, not because they were Jews, but for the same reason and in the same way that obtrusive and objectionable parties of Christians are often objected to in such places (ibid., p. 97).

The president of the University of Virginia had this unsolicited advice for Jews: "Let your people become known for culture as well as for business sagacity, for refinements of speech and manners, for those gracious qualities that have been in all ages the outcome of intimacy with literature and art, and they will not lack sympathy and regard from all members of society who care for the best that is in man" (ibid., p. 102).

A professor from Harvard answered in a similar vein: "Many Jews have personal and social qualities and habits that are unpleasant. . . . These come in large measure from the social isolation to which they have been subjected for centuries, by the prejudice and ignorance of Christian communities. Most Jews are socially untrained, and their bodily habits are not good" (ibid., p. 106). From the president of Tufts University: "The social characteristics of the Jews are peculiar. The subtle thing which we call manners, among them differs from the manners of Americans generally" (ibid., p. 104).

These men would have been indignant if their remarks had been construed as prejudiced, for they repudiated prejudice as un-Christian and irrational. They were convinced that their opinions on Jews were based not on myths or religious invective, but on social reality. As a dean of Columbia wrote in 1904: "What most people regard as a racial problem is really a social problem" (Keppel, 1914, p. 180).

Indeed, to a certain extent, it *was* a social problem, involving real differences in "the subtle thing which we call manners." It would be simplistic to attribute the religious antagonisms of the period solely to bigotry handed down from the past. But it would be equally naïve to assume that class and ethnic differences alone explain the unfavorable attitudes toward Jews that prevailed in academic circles. If not for the history of virulent anti-Semitism and the various stigmas attached to Jews, their cultural peculiarities would have received less notice. Besides, even Jews from respectable backgrounds with "proper" manners were victims of social discrimination. The tendency was to think of all Jews in terms of the immigrant, and to think of all non-Jews in terms of the highest standards of gentility and Christian virture.

During the 1910s there was increasing pressure in certain Eastern colleges to control the Jewish influx. The Jewish "takeover" of City College, which by then was over 80 percent Jewish, served as a warning. Other factors were also at work. World War I fanned the flames of nationalism, and a combination of political demagoguery and nativist propaganda heightened anti-Jewish feeling. For largely independent reasons, the mood inside the colleges was also undergoing change. Reaction was setting in against the reforms of the past 20 years—the expansion of enrollment, the subordination of the classical subjects to science and vocational training, and the related trend toward increased class and ethnic heterogeneity in the student population. Soon after his inauguration as president of Harvard in 1909, Abbott Lawrence Lowell complained that Harvard men were not as intellectually or socially rounded as they ought to be, or by implication, as they once were.

From the turn of the century there were colleges that limited their Jewish enrollment. Beginning around 1920, however, some of the Eastern colleges that previously had been open to Jews adopted policies designed to reduce their Jewish enrollment. To the public, and possibly to themselves, they maintained the illusion of nondiscriminatory admissions. But in fact quotas were instituted, though concealed behind a number of subterfuges. Some colleges set up alumni committees to screen candidates, a device that passed on the onus of religious discrimination to agreeable alumni. Other colleges limited their total enrollment and employed waiting lists that permitted a biased selection of students. Still others, under the pretext of seeking a regional balance, gave preference to students outside the East and thereby limited the number of Jews, almost all of whom lived in the East.

The most common ploy for excluding Jews was the introduction of character tests and psychological exams ("May Jews Go to College?," 1922, p. 708). Before the 1920s, only criteria of scholastic performance were used in the admissions process; now admissions boards began to scrutinize the "outside" interests of students. In addition, school principals were asked to rank students on such characteristics as "fair play," "public spirit," "interest in fellows," and "leadership." These traits were exactly opposite those generally ascribed to Jews. According to the prevailing image, Jews did not use "fair play" but employed unfair methods to get ahead. "Public spirit" and "interest in fellows" were Christian virtues; Jews were outsiders who cared only for themselves. "Leadership" was seen as a prerogative of non-Jews; Jews exhibiting this quality would be regarded as "pushy." School principals, who were invariably Protestant and middle-class, could be expected to reflect these stereotypes in evaluating their Jewish students.

It is not possible to determine precisely how prevalent quotas were during the 1920s, though writers of the period give the impression that by 1930 most private colleges with a large and growing Jewish enrollment had instituted some kind of restrictive device. The most dramatic reversal occurred at Columbia, where the Jewish enrollment declined from 40 to 22 percent in a two-year period *(New York Times,* Jan. 23, 1923, p. 22; Broun & Britt, 1931, p. 74). New York University was also reported to have sharply reduced the number of Jewish students (Broun & Britt, 1931, p. 108). In 1922 a dean explained NYU's policy of selective admissions in this way: "We do not exclude students of any race or national origin because they are foreign, but whenever the student body is found to contain elements from any source in such proportions as to threaten our capacity for assimilating them, we seek by selection to restore the balance" (ibid.). By 1920 Harvard's Jewish enrollment reached 20 percent; no restrictions were yet in effect. Syracuse was roughly 15 percent Jewish in 1923 though the chancellor had to fight off an attempt to "rid the hill of Jews" (ibid.). In 1930 Rutgers admitted only 33 Jewish students in order to "equalize the proportion" in the college. Rumor had it that Princeton used a quota based on the percentage of Jews in the United States; whether true or not, the proportion of Jewish students was minuscule. At Dartmouth in 1930 it was just 7 percent.

It is evident that a tide of bigotry swept college campuses during the 1920s, just as in the nation as a whole. Yet the extent and significance of quotas should not be exaggerated. For one thing, they were confined geographically to the East and, what is more important, to private schools. Second, as objectionable as quotas were, they stopped far short of excluding Jews altogether. If excluded from the elite Eastern colleges, Jewish students could, and did, go elsewhere. [11] Jews had the bitter experience of being treated as outcasts, and some had to settle for a less prestigious education, but in the final analysis the quotas of the 1920s did not constitute a major obstacle to Jewish aspirations.

THE HARVARD AFFAIR

So long as quotas were administered surreptitiously, they were difficult to combat. Few people, least of all Jews, were deceived by the subterfuges that colleges employed, but these methods were effective in preventing public exposure and political agitation. This situation was suddenly changed with a terse announcement issued by Harvard University in June 1922. The full text reads as follows:

The great increase which has recently taken place in the number of students at Harvard College, as at the other colleges, has brought up forcibly the problem of the limitation of enrollment.

We have not at present sufficient classrooms or dormitories, especially freshman dormitories, to take care of any further large increase. This problem is really a group of problems, all difficult, and most of them needing for their settlement more facts than we now have. Before a general policy can be formulated on this great question it must engage the attention of the Governing Board and the Faculties and it is likely to be discussed by alumni and undergraduates.

It is natural that with a widespread discussion of this sort going on there should be talk about the proportion of Jews at the college At present the whole problem of limitation of enrollment is in the stage of general discussion and it may remain in that stage for a considerable time (*New York Times,* June 2, 1922, p. 1, italics added).

[11] "That the situation was far from desperate is indicated by the fact that in the twenties there was no flight of Northern Jews to the unrestricted state universities of the lower South and the trans-Mississippi West; Jewish enrollments there remained very slight" (Higham, 1957, p. 22). Substantiating data are reported in Broun and Britt (1931, Ch. 4).

Why did Harvard not proceed more discreetly and simply adopt the subterfuges employed elsewhere? The reason is to be found in the personality of President Lowell, perhaps in his New England candor, more likely in his naïveté and underlying prejudice. Lowell believed that he was acting courageously. As he wrote on one occasion: "This question is with us. We cannot solve it by forgetting or ignoring it" (*New York Times,* June 17, 1922, p. 1). In his commencement address a week later he added a touch of eloquence: "To shut the eyes to an actual problem of this kind and ignore its existence, or to refuse to grapple with it courageously, would be unworthy of a university" (*New York Times,* June 23, 1922, p. 1). The "problem" was that Jewish enrollment at Harvard had increased from 6 percent in 1908 to 20 percent in 1922. Lowell, however, was determined to avoid the "indirect methods" employed elsewhere (*New York Times,* June 17, 1922, p. 3). The storm of protest that ensued must have given him occasion to question the practicality of such moral rectitude.

Elected officials were among the first to react. On the day after the papers reported the news from Harvard, a state legislator from Massachusetts proposed a bill for a legislative inquiry. On the next day President Lowell traveled to the State House where he conferred privately with the Speaker of the House of Representatives. The Speaker obliged Lowell with a public statement that dismissed the press report as "idle rumor," adding that "Harvard would remain, as in the past, a great university for all the people . . ." (*New York Times,* June 4, 1922, p. 18). Nevertheless, the protest in the state legislature continued unabated. One pending bill proposed to eliminate all reference to Harvard University from the state constitution in order to disassociate the state from Harvard's discriminatory policies. Another proposal called for a review of the tax exemptions that Harvard enjoyed on its property. The Boston City Council passed its own resolution condemning the Harvard administration. Finally, the Governor appointed a committee to investigate possible discrimination at Harvard. The *New York Times* reported that Harvard officials were "surprised" since they had assumed that "any plan for a State investigation would die a natural death" (*New York Times,* June 7, 1922, p. 1).

This was an impressive response from the official sector, unusual for the 1920s. Nevertheless, the resolute president of

Harvard stood his ground. An exchange of letters with a dissenting Jewish alumnus was printed in the *New York Times* (June 17, 1922, p. 1). Lowell's letter began with the disclaimer that "there is perhaps no body of men in the United States . . . with so little anti-Semitic feeling as the instructing staff of Harvard University." The letter continued: "There is, most unfortunately, a rapidly growing anti-Semitic feeling in this country . . . fraught with very great evils for the Jews, and very great perils for the community." Finally the logic becomes clear: quotas are designed not to harm Jews, but to reduce anti-Semitism. They were in the best interests of Jews themselves:

The anti-Semitic feeling among the students is increasing, and it grows in proportion to the increase in the number of Jews. If their number should become 40 percent of the student body, the race feeling would become intense. When on the other hand, the number of Jews was small, the race antagonism was small also. . . . If every college in the country would take a limited proportion of Jews, I suspect we should go a long way toward eliminating race feeling among the students, and as these students passed out into the world, eliminating it in the community.

For President Lowell, restricting Jewish enrollment at Harvard was a way of restricting the growth of anti-Semitism. His Jewish correspondent was unconvinced: "If it be true . . . that the anti-Semitic feeling among the students is increasing, should it not be the function of an institution of learning to discourage rather than encourage such a spirit?"

The criticism that was marshaled against President Lowell and Harvard owed itself in part to the political influence that Jews enjoyed both within and outside the university. The Jewish concentration in and around Boston was given further significance by gerrymandering practices that drew political boundaries so as to maximize ethnic homogeneity. As a consequence there were a number of "Jewish districts" that elected Jewish candidates to the state legislature. This was at least one factor in the strong action that state and city officials took against Harvard's proposed quotas.

In addition, Jews were strategically located within the power structure of the university. First, there were the Jewish alumni, like the one quoted above, who were outspoken in their opposition to quotas. Second, Harvard's governing body, the Board of

Overseers, had one Jewish member, Judge Julian W. Mack of Chicago, a leader in the American Jewish Congress. According to one newspaper report, he was "much exercized over the matter" (*New York Times,* June 6, 1922, p. 1).

A third political resource was the small number of Jewish faculty at Harvard. When President Lowell appointed a committee of thirteen to review the college's admissions policies, it included three Jews. All had German names, and judging from the committee's final report, it is doubtful that they did much to defend Jewish interests. Nevertheless, the mere presence of Jews on the faculty and through the ranks of the college made it all the more difficult to justify the sudden imposition of quotas.

Student opinion at Harvard was divided. A professor of social ethics asked his class to discuss whether religious restrictions were ethically justified. In the class of 83, 41 defended religious quotas. Thirty-four, including seven with Jewish names, held that such a policy was not justifiable; the remaining eight were undecided (Ham, 1922, pp. 225–227).

Some students who defended quotas expressed resentment of Jewish academic success: "They memorize their books! Thus they keep the average of scholarship so high that others with a high degree of common sense, but less parrot-knowledge, are prevented from attaining a representative grade." A second criticism was that Jews were clannish and did not fit into student life: "They do not mix. They destroy the unity of the college." "They are governed by selfishness." "Jews are an unassimilable race, as dangerous to a college as indigestible food to a man." Other responses were not explicitly anti-Jewish. A few expressed the view that Harvard's founding fathers "wanted certain traditions maintained and it is a duty to maintain them. . . ." A more common argument was that "Harvard must maintain a cosmopolitan balance."

As these comments suggest, the arguments in defense of quotas were basically of two kinds. One pointed to objectionable traits of Jews; the other pointed to desirable traits of the university that were presumably endangered. The latter argument did not accuse Jews of any objectionable behavior, but assumed the *absence* of qualities necessary for the preservation of the institution's special character. This view was expressed by some of the leading journals of the day. One writer commented that Jewish immigrants "had little training in the amenities and delicacies of civilized existence," and if the proportion of Jews at Harvard increased to 40 percent as President Lowell warned, "this means that its character would be completely changed" ("The Jews and the Colleges," 1922, p. 353). Another journal was more forceful:

It is one of the severest and most distressing tasks of college authorities today to exercise that discrimination which will keep college ideals and atmosphere pure and sound and yet not quench this eager spirit. . . . Racial and religious oppression and prejudice have no place in America, and least of all in academic environments. But the effort to maintain standards against untrained minds and spirits is not oppression or prejudice ("Exclusion from College," 1922, p. 407).

Even the *Nation,* in commenting on the genteel tradition at Harvard, Yale, and Princeton, conceded that "the infiltration of a mass of pushing young men with a foreign accent accustomed to overcome discrimination by self-assertiveness would obviously change the character of any of these institutions and lessen its social prestige" ("May Jews Go to College?" 1922, p. 708). However, the *Nation*'s editorial did not defend quotas. It was resigned to the inevitability that "some of the beauty of the aristocratic tradition" would be lost, but argued that America should not imitate the methods of "the most backward in Europe." As might be expected, Jewish opinion challenged the legitimacy of judging applicants in terms of character as well as intelligence. As one Jewish writer put it: "We think that a university which keeps a man out because it doesn't like his character is almost as benighted as the one which would sift him out because he is a Jew" ("Harvard 'Talk' about Jews," 1922, p. 28).

"*Almost* as benighted." It was difficult to deny the difference between rejecting applicants on sheer religious grounds and rejecting them because they lacked a preferred set of social characteristics. Advocates of quotas did not question the right of Jews to a college education. Rather the issue was the right of certain Eastern colleges to preserve their unique character, which was Protestant and upper-class. The problem was not simply that Jews were displacing upper-class Protestants. More important was the effect that this had for the reputation of the college. City College was stigmatized as "the Jewish University of America," and the University of Pennsylvania was said to have "the democracy of the street car" (Veysey, 1965, p. 288). As these colleges suffered in prestige, they ceased to attract students from prestigious families. The influx of Jews did in fact constitute a threat to the character of the elite colleges so long as their character was defined in elite terms.

One might assume that the president of Harvard was motivated by a sincere desire to preserve Harvard's historic identity rather than by anti-Semitism. After all, was he not the president of an institution with a reputation for liberalism and tolerance? Was this not the A. Lawrence Lowell who in 1902 warned his predecessor of the "great danger of a snobbish separation of the students on lines of wealth" and who, in his own administration, had constructed compulsory freshman dormitories and commons (Earnest, 1953, p. 216)? And did not President Lowell, in the same commencement address in which he defended his proposal for selective admissions, also express the view that "Americanization does not mean merely molding them [foreigners] to an already settled type, but the blending together of many distinct elements . . . [each] with qualities which can enrich our common heritage" (*New York Times,* June 23, 1922, p. 1). Certainly there were good grounds, both democratic and academic, for opposing President Lowell's proposed quotas. But at least his motives seemed unimpeachable.

Considerable doubt, however, is cast on Lowell's motives by an incident that occurred on Christmas day, 1922, six months after the Harvard address. Traveling on the New York–New Haven railroad, President Lowell was engaged in conversation by a man—Victor Albert Kramer—who, unbeknownst to Lowell, was both Jewish and a graduate of Harvard. Several weeks later, at a synagogue forum on discrimination against Negroes, Kramer described his encounter with President Lowell. Thanks to the presence of a *New York Times* reporter, the event was reported in the press (*New York Times,* Jan. 16, 1923, p. 23).

According to Kramer, Lowell predicted a worsening of conditions for Jews so long as they remained apart and resisted intermarriage. Jews had outworn their religion, he believed, and must give up their peculiar practices if they expected to be treated with equality. The man who had publicly extolled the contributions each immigrant group could make to the evolving American now in private conversation asserted that a Jew could not be both a Jew and an American. Finally, he expressed satisfaction in the fact that New York University had reduced Jewish enrollment and took credit for Harvard's plan to do likewise. [12]

Lowell never denied the encounter on the train, though a statement issued by his office claimed that the newspaper report "grossly misrepresents his views." The statement continued sanctimoniously: "His earnest desire is to see anti-Semitic prejudice and Semitic segregation abolished in this country, and he believes that Jews and Gentiles should work together to this end . . ." (*New York Times,* Jan. 16, 1923, p. 23). In Lowell's view "Semitic segregation" stirred up latent anti-Semitic prejudice. A ceiling on the number of Jews at Harvard was therefore in the interest of both groups.

While President Lowell disapproved of "Semitic segregation," he was of a different opinion with respect to Negroes. Even before becoming president, Lowell expressed his dislike for the residential separation between Harvard's wealthy students, who resided in lavish apartments known as the Gold Coast, and the less privileged students. His construction of compulsory freshman dormitories earned him a reputation as a champion of democracy. Less often mentioned is that Lowell also instituted a color ban. Freshman dormitories were compulsory for everyone but the handful of Harvard's black students. For them it was compulsory to find living quarters elsewhere.

Like the proposed religious quotas, the color ban became a cause célèbre. Negro civil rights groups agitated against it and 149 Harvard alumni signed a protest petition, but to no avail. As Lowell wrote in a letter to the father of one of Harvard's black freshmen:

. . . I am sorry to have to tell you that in the Freshman Halls, where residence is compulsory, we have felt from the beginning the necessity of not including colored men. To the other dormitories and dining rooms they are admitted freely, but in the Freshman Halls I am sure you will understand why . . . we have not thought it possible to compel men of different races to reside together (*New York Times,* Jan. 12, 1923, p. 5).

---

[12] In personal communication, Mr. Kramer has confirmed the accuracy of the original *Times* report of his conversation with President Lowell. Kramer also published his account of the incident in the *American Hebrew,* Jan. 26, 1923.

Lowell's correspondent was himself a Harvard graduate and his son had received his previous schooling at fashionable Exeter Academy. There is more than irony in this. If Harvard chose to discriminate it was not in response to a conflict between two cultures. The only sense in which there was a clash of values was that racial prejudice itself was part of upper-class Protestant society.

The exposure of Lowell's underlying bigotry does not by itself invalidate the arguments put forward in defense of quotas or discredit those who sought to preserve Harvard's aristocratic traditions. However, it does point up the tenuousness of the distinction between base prejudice, on the one hand, and protection of cultural values, on the other. One has to be wary that the defense for quotas, as formulated by educators and journalists, was not merely a sophisticated rationale for ordinary prejudice.

The basic truth is that racial and religious prejudice was one of the underpinnings of upper-class society. On the surface, upper-class Protestants may have been protecting their status prerogatives and their cultural symbols. But prejudice was a factor in the very definition of status, just as it was a factor in the choice of cultural symbols. Harvard was elite not simply because it was upper-class and genteel, but also because it was predominantly white and Protestant. In the final analysis, the lower-class origins and ethnic peculiarities of Jews were only of secondary importance. Given the climate of intolerance that characterized the 1920s, the class character of higher education, and the fact that upwardly mobile Jews were penetrating one of the most sacred institutions of the Protestant establishment, Jews would have aroused anatagonism no matter what their level of assimilation. As Horace Kallen wrote in 1923: ". . . it is not the failure of Jews to be assimilated into undergraduate society which troubles them [President Lowell and his defenders]. They do not want Jews to be assimilated into undergraduate society. What troubles them is the completeness with which the Jews want to be and have been assimilated" (Kallen, 1923, p. 242).

REGIONAL QUOTAS The debate over quotas languished for several months. However, almost all the political agitation was confined to a five-day period that began with the Harvard announcement raising the possibility of quotas and ended with a decision by the college's Board of Overseers to refer the issue to a special faculty committee. When the board dramatically met in emergency session and announced that no changes in the college's entrance requirements would be made until after the committee had reported, the opponents of quotas probably assumed that the administration was on the retreat. Whether by design or not, however, the committee only functioned as a protective screen for the administration. It removed the issue of quotas from the public arena and insulated Harvard's officialdom from public scrutiny and political pressure. Almost a year passed before the committee issued its report. Its conclusions were probably foreshadowed by the very instructions given to the committee: "To consider . . . principles and methods for more effective sifting of candidates for admission to the university" (Report of the Committee . . . 1923).

The six-page report issued by the committee was unequivocal in repudiating quotas as inconsistent with Harvard's tradition of "equal opportunity for all regardless of race and religion." Indeed, the authors of the report seemed to go out of their way to avoid any proposal that might be construed by suspicious minds as prejudiced: "Even so rational a method as a personal conference or an intelligence test, if now adopted here as a means of selection, would inevitably be regarded as a covert device to eliminate those deemed racially or socially undesirable. . . ."

The report did not stop here, however. The committee's assigned task was not simply to study religious quotas, but to review *all* of Harvard's admissions procedures. This the committee did with apparent good conscience. It announced its opposition to the policy of giving preference to the sons of graduates and recommended several minor changes in the college's entrance requirements that were intended to upgrade the student body. The reforms, the report asserted, "would solve one part of our problem."

The report continued: "The other part of the problem, namely the building up of a new group of men from the West and South and, in general, from good high schools in towns and small cities, is more difficult." The difficulty was that students from these regions did not receive a high school education that prepared them for Harvard College. As a consequence they were unable to pass Harvard's entrance examination. The committee's solution was to waive the entrance examination for students in the highest seventh of their graduating class if they had completed an approved course of study and had the recommendation of their school. The committee reasoned that such students had demonstrated their fitness within their own schools, and that "the best product is likely to succeed in college better than the poorer portion of the group admitted under our present examinations." On this assumption the committee felt confident that Harvard's standards would not be lowered by accepting students who could not pass the usual entrance examination.

The men who drafted this proposal must have been aware that, if implemented, it would drastically alter the religious composition of Harvard's undergraduates. Jews were overwhelmingly concentrated in the urban centers on the Eastern seaboard, and "to raise the proportion of country boys and students from the interior" would obviously reduce the Jewish representation. Other Eastern colleges had already employed this as a strategy for excluding Jews. Between 1920 and 1922 Columbia instituted regional quotas, with the result that the Jewish proportion at the college was cut in half, from 40 to 22 percent.[13] Although no comparable figures are available for Harvard, there is no reason to think that its motives were different. It was not until the influx of Jewish students that Eastern colleges began to worry about achieving a "regional balance," and it was not until the crisis over Harvard's proposed quotas that a student's geographical backgound was deemed relevant to his admission to the college.

A policy of recruiting nationally can be, and often is, defended on legitimate grounds. It is said to increase the quality of the student body, to diversify and enrich student culture, and to extend the influence of the college. Whatever merit these arguments have, the concept of "regional balance" originated as a rationale for discrimination. Its application has had the aim and the result of restricting Jewish enrollment and protecting the status claims of the elite Eastern colleges.

CONCLUSION   Jewish immigrants entered a situation of expanding educational opportunity. They arrived at a time when American higher education was growing at an unprecedented rate, and despite problems they encountered in the elite colleges, few obstacles blocked the

[13] When accused of discrimination Columbia's administration conceded that that there had been a "decrease in the number of Jewish students in the last three years," but attributed it to a "natural change in the geographical distribution for the student body" (*New York Times,* Jan. 23, 1923, p. 22).

path of aspiring Jewish students. Jews were strategically located in the urban centers in the East, close to the nation's leading educational institutions, and also had easy access to public institutions, such as City College, which provided tens of thousands of second- and third-generation Jews with a free education.

Even more important is the fact that the structure and content of higher education were changing in directions that corresponded with Jewish interests and talents. Had the average college curriculum retained its emphasis on Latin, Greek, and other classical subjects, it is doubtful whether the children of Jewish immigrants would have distinguished themselves academically. As Chapter 6 shows, even today Jewish representation in the humanities and the fine arts is relatively low; it is in fields developed since the beginning of the century—especially the social sciences and certain of the professions—that Jews have been most prominent.

Inasmuch as Jews displayed an enthusiasm for education and a capacity for academic excellence, they were the "right" people to take advantage of expanding educational opportunities. But Jews also had the good fortune of being in the "right" place at the "right" time. No other ethnic group in America has found itself in such fortuitous circumstances when it was prepared for its breakthrough into higher education.

2. American Catholicism and the "School Question"

In 1904 a Catholic archbishop expressed his opposition to public education in these uncompromising terms: ". . . let us have no deal, no alliance with the promoters of godless education, either in the primary schools, or in the intermediate schools, or in the universities. At every stage, we must have God, and Christ, and the Pope, and our ancient faith, no matter what the consequences" (Meyer, 1907, p. 167). Such hostility toward public education has been a prominent feature of Catholicism in America and undoubtedly has had far-reaching consequences given the importance of the educational institutions as a channel of class mobility. The Catholic reaction against public education has also affected the quality of intellectual life in the Church and among its adherents. Writing in 1963, Richard Hofstadter scored Catholics for having "failed to develop an intellectual tradition in America or to produce its own class of intellectuals . . ." (Hofstadter, 1963, p. 136). Indeed, studies ranging over several decades have shown a pattern of Catholic underrepresentation among the nation's scientists and scholars. Other studies have reported a low level of academic productivity in Catholic colleges.[1]

From the earliest days of public education it was apparent that Catholics would be at odds with the nation's educational institutions. The architects of the common school idealistically viewed it as a liberating force that would spread enlightenment, produce an informed electorate, and eliminate social inequality. Jewish immigrants would later see it as an unprecedented opportunity to participate in the life of the society in which they lived. For Catholics, however, the common school raised a great question. One archbishop called it "the most living question of our day and for our

---

[1] Huntington and Whitney (1927); Lehman and Witty (1931); Knapp and Goodrich (1952); Knapp and Greenbaum (1953).

33

people" (Cross, 1968, p. 130). The question was whether public education would subvert the faith and morals of Catholic children. On a more practical level the question was whether the Church should discourage or even prohibit Catholic parents from sending their children to public schools, and whether the Church should develop a system of parish schools.

What were the sources of Catholic hostility to public education? Why did Catholics feel compelled to relinquish their right to a free education and undertake the enormous costs of developing a separate system of parochial schools? Why have Catholics failed to produce their share of scholars and scientists? Does the fault lie within Catholicism, perhaps in a native anti-intellectualism, as some critics have implied, or are the causes to be found in social conditions that were peculiar to nineteenth- and early twentieth-century America? The answers to these questions are not only important in themselves, but will provide a basis for understanding why the rates of scholarly productivity among Catholics are higher now than in the past.

A LEGACY OF BIGOTRY In the most general sense, the Catholic commitment to parochial education was a response to the fact that the surrounding society, including its schools, was Protestant. There was a great deal in nineteenth-century America to remind Catholics of this fact.

First of all, there was the legacy of anti-Catholic prejudice that was older than the country itself. The colonial settlers left England before it had recovered from the scars of the Reformation. Not only did these settlers carry with them a deep-seated anti-Catholicism, but once in America they were removed from the liberal currents that gradually diminished anti-Catholic feeling in Europe (Billington, 1964, p. 4). Furthermore, many of the Protestant settlers were themselves refugees from religious persecution and sought to establish religious colonies in the New World where they could pursue their religious doctrines without interference or competition from others. This combination of religious fervor and native anti-Catholicism resulted in the persecution of Catholics, frequently under the sanction of law. According to one historian, "By 1700 a Catholic could enjoy full civil and religious rights only in Rhode Island" (ibid., p. 9). It is no exaggeration to say that anti-Catholicism was part of the political and cultural fabric of the new nation.

The position of Catholics improved at the end of the eighteenth century. With independence, confidence grew that the political and religious destiny of the nation had been established, and most legal restrictions on Catholics were abrogated. Furthermore, the tide of immigration was largely Protestant, and Catholics were an insignificant proportion of the population. In 1790 there were only 35,000 Catholics in the United States, constituting only 1 percent of the total population. For these reasons Protestant-Catholic conflict was at low ebb at the turn of the nineteenth century. The situation was like that which existed for German Jews prior to the Eastern European immigration. But it was also similar in that the climate of tolerance was a precarious one. Anti-Catholic stereotypes and sentiments were present in the culture, and were easily reactivated with the immigration of over a million Irish Catholics beginning in the 1840s.

Irish immigration marked several firsts in American immigration history, none of them auspicious for the acceptance of Irish into American society. For one thing, Irish immigration was unprecedented in sheer magnitude. Prior to 1840 the number of arrivals from all countries never exceeded 30,000 in any single year. During the early 1840s Irish immigration began to gain momentum. A drop in the price of grain on European markets induced landowners to shift from farming to grazing, and in the process millions of tenant farmers were ruthlessly evicted from their homes. But the real upsurge in immigration was triggered by the potato rot, which began in 1845 and lasted for five years. In 1851, the peak year of Irish immigration, 221,000 Irish entered the country. The total for the eight-year period from 1847 to 1854 was 1,187,000 (*Reports of the Immigration Commission,* vol. 1, 1911, pp. 66–96). Never before had the nation absorbed such a concentrated wave of immigrants.

The fact that the Irish who came during this period were impoverished and famine-stricken constitutes a second difference. Although indigents and indentured servants figured in earlier immigration, their numbers were small and offset by a more respectable class of immigrants who came with surplus cash or occupational skills. Despite their rural backgrounds, the Irish lacked even agricultural skills since most had worked as field laborers and not as independent farmers. This is the main reason they remained in the cities in the Northeast, not because they lacked money to travel into America's heartland as is often suggested.

Lacking industrial skills, the Irish were confined to the lowest occupations. Census data indicate that with few exceptions men worked as common laborers and women as domestics (Ernst, 1965, pp. 214–217). The combined effect of poverty and discrimination was that the Irish crowded together in the least desirable neighborhoods. For the first time the nation had ethnic slums, replete with high rates of pauperism, disease, and crime. Popular opinion was further aroused by the increased costs of running public agencies such as hospitals, poorhouses, and prisons (Handlin, 1968).

The third and most important way in which the Irish differed from previous immigrants is that after 1840 almost all of them were Catholic. Furthermore they were intensely, almost militantly Catholic as a result of centuries of religious persecution by the English. American Protestants, themselves deeply religious, reacted with almost paranoic fear to what was perceived as a papal invasion. As one historian writes:

The erection of Catholic churches and the establishment of convents was a most terrifying thing to the intensely Protestant Americans. The possibility of the Pope's colonizing America with Catholics in order to extend his authority over the republic was very real in the minds of many earnest people. To what purpose, they asked, were Catholics flocking into the police forces of our cities, enlisting in military organizations, and storing firearms in the basements of Catholic churches if a day of reckoning between Protestants and Catholics was not near at hand? (Stephenson, 1926, p. 100).

Even though such fears were obviously exaggerated, the size of the Irish influx did mean that the Protestant character of the nation's institutions would inevitably be challenged for the first time. Protestant reaction was also inevitable, especially given the destitution and the accompanying social problems in areas of high Irish concentration.

These factors help to explain the resurgence of anti-Catholic prejudice during the nineteenth century. Occasionally prejudice flared into violence, as when a Boston convent was burned in 1834 or when anti-Irish mobs ravaged Philadelphia for three days in 1844, leaving 13 dead. The more important development, however, was the emergence of a nativist movement that won control of a number of state governments in both the North and South. While the Know-Nothings made surprisingly little headway in enacting their anti-Catholic program, they intensified and politicized the cleavages that already existed between Protestants and Catholics.

The Irish had virtually become a caste in relation to the rest of society—stigmatized, spatially isolated, and relegated to inferior status positions. At the same time prejudice had the effect of reinforcing ethnic and religious solidarity. By mid-century the lines between Irish Catholics and Protestants were clearly drawn. Both lived in separate communities and between them was a chasm of mutual suspicion and enmity.

The conflict over the schools can only be understood within this broad context of Protestant-Catholic division. To balk at relinquishing control over the education of their children to the state was, at least in part, an expression of the alienation that Irish felt toward a political system they had reason to distrust. To build a separate system of education that would be sensitive to their own culture and religion was consistent with the general position of Irish in relation to the larger society. Having built their own churches, charities, self-help organizations, fraternal associations, and cultural institutions, did it not also make sense to build their own schools?

ETHNIC SOLIDARITY Although anti-Catholic bigotry helped to foster a spirit of independence among Catholic immigrants, a much stronger incentive for establishing parochial schools stemmed from a desire to preserve ethnicity. To a very large extent parochial schools were the creations of immigrant communities concerned with their survival. As Philip Gleason writes in his article on "Immigration and American Catholic Intellectual Life":

> For the Catholic ethnic groups, religion was an essential part of the cultural heritage they wished to pass on to their children, but it was not the whole of the heritage. The schools they set up performed the functions, in addition to intellectual and religious training, of transmitting the ancestral language, orienting the young to the national symbols of the group, and preserving the identity and continuity of the group through successive generations. *Intellectual excellence was not the only, or even the primary consideration; rather, intellectual and religious interests had, as it were, to compete with national and group interests* (Gleason, 1964, p. 160, italics added).

In the case of the Irish, religious and national identity had been welded together through centuries of political domination and religious oppression by the English. Irish nationalism ran deep, and as one writer observes, "the parochial school was a self-contained social system from which Irish solidarity drew much of its strength" (Levine, 1966, p. 831).

German Catholics, given their strong nationalistic sentiments, also tended to regard ethnic and religious identity as inseparable. They believed that the preservation of faith depended upon the preservation of German pride and the German language in particular. Parochial schools under German control could therefore protect ethnicity and religion at one and the same time. As Robert Cross (1968, p. 91) writes: "The Germans believed that only a clergy proud of its origins would be able to hold adult German Catholics in the faith, and that only parochial schools in which German was the dominant language would save the children from demoralization and deCatholicization." The view of German Catholics was summed up in the slogan: "Language Saves Faith" (Barry, 1953, p. 10).

In their study of *The Polish Peasant in Europe and America,* Thomas and Znaniecki (1927, p. 50) also viewed the parochial school as an instrument of ethnic survival:

Good or bad, the parochial school is a social product of the immigrant and satisfies important needs of the latter. The most essential point is neither the religious character of the parochial school, nor even the fact that it serves to preserve in the young generation the language and cultural traditions of the old country; it is the function of the parochial school as a factor of the social unity of the immigrant colony and of its continuity through successive generations. . . .

Thomas and Znaniecki found that—unlike the children who attended public school—parochial school children were not estranged from their parents and from their native culture.

A study of Chicago's Italian community between 1880 and 1930 also observed that part of the attraction of parochial schools was that children could learn to write and read Italian (Nelli, 1970, p. 67). Even as late as 1958, in his study of an Italian ghetto in Boston, Herbert Gans found that Italians feared that public education undermined ethnic solidarity: " . . . parents are suspicious that education will estrange the children from them, and from the peer group society as well. Consequently, they are somewhat fearful about the public education to which the children are exposed in high school" (Gans, 1962, p. 128).

The importance of ethnic factors in the development of parochial schools is highlighted by the fact that in communities where an ethnic mixture existed among Catholics, it was common practice for each group to build its own parochial school. When this was not possible, Catholic parents often preferred public schools to parochial schools controlled by some other nationality group. For example, this was the case among Irish and Italians living in Greenwich Village during the 1920s. According to an early study, "The Italians mostly sent their children to the public schools while nearly all the Irish attended parochial schools. In the few cases where Irish and Italian children were not trained in different systems, they attended different schools" (Ware, 1965, p. 320). Often parochial schools existed for the purpose of preserving an immigrant group's native language; a 1916 study of 52 parochial schools found that 30 could be classified as foreign language schools (Miller, 1916, p. 32). In Burlington, Vermont, during the 1930s the situation was reversed. Since the parochial schools were controlled by the Irish, most French-Canadians sent their children to the public schools where they could learn French (Anderson, 1937, Ch. 7).

If ethnic purposes and functions were central to the parochial schools, why were parochial schools organized along religious rather than ethnic lines? One obvious factor was that the Church alone had the organization and the resources to undertake such a monumental task. Another factor was that American society was actively committed to a policy of Americanization, and establishing schools along nationality lines would have gone against powerful ideological currents opposed to "colonization." However, whereas native Americans might not tolerate ethnic schools, constitutional guarantees of religious freedom made it difficult to oppose schools created on a religious basis, at least if they were privately funded. Hence, in their religion, Irish, Italian, German, and Polish immigrants found a legitimate basis for establishing schools that would allow them to pass on their native culture to the next generation.

Nevertheless, the concern for ethnic survival by itself would not have been sufficient to induce Catholics to build a separate school system. After all, Catholics did participate in other institutional spheres of American society, and other immigrant groups, most notably Jews, were not deterred from public education despite their apprehensions about assimilation. In addition to the various ethnic factors that have been examined, there were unique religious sources for Catholic disenchantment with public education.

PROTES-TANTISM IN THE SCHOOLS American institutions have always had a Protestant cast, hardly surprising given the Protestant origins of the nation and the preponderance of Protestants in the population. But early in the nineteenth century the Protestant character of public institutions was far from subtle. Protestant ministers typically had exclusive access to public institutions, such as hospitals, prisons, poorhouses, asylums, and orphanages (Handlin, 1968, pp. 167–168). Even when these institutions ministered mainly to Catholic immigrants, Protestants were unwilling to relinquish control. In Boston, for example, Catholic priests were not admitted to state institutions until 1879 (ibid., p. 215). Especially for devout Catholics who depended on the ministrations of a priest in times of personal crisis, this was a grave matter. Catholics were reinforced in their belief that life in a Protestant society was problematic, and they proceeded with urgency to develop their own welfare agencies.

Nowhere was Protestant control more firmly entrenched than in the schools. The public, nonsectarian education of the late nineteenth century was an outgrowth of the private church schools of the eighteenth century. As one historian writes: "During the Colonial period the association between education and religion in aim, content, method, and control had been quite close, both in public mind and official act" (Monroe, 1940, p. 265). At the turn of the nineteenth century most schools were either private schools for the privileged or charity schools operated by local churches; in both cases religious influences were very strong. Public funding was virtually nonexistent, as the designation of *charity schools* would suggest.

During the early part of the nineteenth century the ideals of free and universal education began to take hold and public funds for education were substantially increased. However, control and administration of public schools were not yet defined as the exclusive responsibility of the state. The historical pattern of religious control continued, with schools operated by religious organizations and benevolent societies. In order to avoid religious dissension, it was generally agreed that the schools would not teach the doctrines of any single denomination or sect, but only elements that were common to all. The end result was a vague but decidedly Protestant atmosphere, evident in the content of prayers, hymns, and religious instruction.

This pattern was established before the upsurge in Catholic immigration, and if not for this development, the Protestant character of public education might have gone unchallenged. Inevitably Catholics resented the Protestant, and sometimes anti-Catholic overtones of the public schools, and in areas with large Catholic concentrations there was movement toward building separate schools. In some places Catholics had no trouble receiving a portion

of the public school fund. However, in other places Catholic re-
quests for a proportionate share of public funds became the subject
of prolonged and acrimonious controversy.

The most bitter and decisive conflict occurred in New York City
between 1840 and 1844.[2] In 1840 most schools in New York City
were under the control of the Public School Society. Founded in
1805 as a private association whose aim was to provide education
for children who could not afford private schools, the society eventually became financed by the state and operated most of the city's
schools. The religious climate it fostered in the schools was unmistakably Protestant. The King James Bible was used in daily
prayers and religious training, and some textbooks contained passages that were blatantly anti-Catholic (Lannie, 1968, Ch. 4).

Ironically, it was not disaffected Catholics but a Whig governor
who brought the issue into the open. In a legislative message in
1840 Governor Seward complained that thousands of immigrant
children were kept away from the schools by the sectarian nature
of their instruction. As a remedy he proposed the "establishment
of schools in which they may be instructed by teachers speaking
the same language with themselves, and professing the same
faith."[3] Encouraged by Seward's proposal, a group of Catholic
churches in New York petitioned the Common Council for a share
of public school funds, but were unanimously rebuffed. The council
argued that such a precedent would eventually result in a system
of sectarian education as other religious groups advanced similar
claims. Of course, in the Catholic view the Public School Society
was already practicing sectarian education.

Public opinion was predictably anti-Catholic and further in-
flamed by tendentious press reports that portrayed Protestants as
the aggrieved party. One newspaper commented: "They demand
of us to take away our children's funds and bestow them on the
subjects of Rome, the creatures of a foreign hierarchy" (Billington,

---

[2] A recent volume devoted entirely to this episode is Lannie (1968). For other
accounts, see Boese (1869); Palmer (1905, Ch. 12); Burns (1908, pp. 360–375);
and Billington (1964, Ch. 6).

[3] Baker (1955, pp. 212–213). Seward was acting less out of sympathy for Catholics than out of concern that an estimated 20,000 children were not receiving
public education. Nor was he in favor of allocating public money to Catholic
schools. On the contrary, he subscribed to the view of the schools as an assimilating agency that would "reduce uncongenial masses into one intelligent,
virtuous, harmonious, and happy people" (p. 218).

1964, p. 148). Fears of Popery and resentment of Catholics for tampering with the schools were widespread. As Billington writes in his history of anti-Catholicism in America: "The sight of a high churchman openly campaigning to secure funds which Protestants believed to be their own was more than many of them could bear, particularly when they believed that [Bishop] Hughes was seeking this money only to spread his papal beliefs" (ibid., p. 148).

Undeterred by public opinion and committed to the principle of state-controlled education, Governor Seward in 1842 proposed legislation to replace the Public School Society with a system of school commissioners elected in each ward. When the final vote came, Democratic legislators supported the proposed reorganization of the schools, mainly as a concession to the growing Catholic voting bloc. On the night the bill passed, mobs attacked Irish immigrants in the streets, and the militia was summoned to protect Catholic churches.[4]

The Catholic victory was a qualified one. The new school law enabled Catholics to implement some changes in wards that they controlled. But Catholics had failed to win their most important objective: public funding of parochial schools. As one writer assesses the aftermath of the New York conflict: "After 1840, when attempts to gain public support for New York parochial schools failed, Catholic interest and energy began to be expended almost exclusively on Catholic parochial and private schools, leaving the public schools as a semi-Protestant domain" (McCluskey, 1964*b*, p. 31).

Catholics had succeeded in wresting control over the schools away from the Public School Society, which on one occasion Bishop Hughes called "a close corporation composed of bigots" (Lannie, 1968, p. 250). However, once control over the schools was invested in the state, it was only a matter of time before the schools would become completely secularized. The prospect of "Godless schools" was no less troublesome to Catholics than the Protestant influences that they had successfully curtailed. In this sense the religious conflict of the first half of the nineteenth century contained the seeds for the conflict of the second half.

---

[4] Conflicts like the one in New York, though less inflammatory, were common after mid-century. For example, in 1856 a ruling of the Maine Supreme Court upheld the right of school authorities to expel a Catholic girl who refused to read the King James Bible, a decision that was not reversed until 1890 (Heath, 1856, pp. 376–413).

NON-
SECTARIAN
SCHOOLS:
DEMOCRATI-
ZATION
OR
ABSORPTION?

The middle of the nineteenth century was a critical juncture in the history of public education, with implications of overwhelming importance not only for Catholics but also for the future of cultural pluralism in America. For the first time the nation was confronted with a sizable non-Protestant minority determined to preserve its cultural and religious identity. Given the significance of the school as an agent of socialization, it inevitably became the battleground where the relation of cultural minorities to the larger body politic would be worked out. Futhermore, the intense religious conflict of the first half of the century made it imperative to find a solution. It was untenable to deny Catholics a share of the public school fund at the same time that Protestants injected their own religion into the educational program. The nation was thus faced with a choice that was simple in theory but complex in its implications.

One alternative was to develop a pluralistic system of education with schools drawn along religious lines, each claiming a proportionate share of the public school fund. Precedents for this arrangement existed in other countries. As Robert Cross (1968, p. 137) writes: "The German government supported Catholic schools with direct grants, and England appropriated to every school a flat sum for each student brought to a given level of intellectual competence. Though either plan was satisfactory, [Church] conservatives, in drawing up an 'ideal school bill,' chose the English plan." Precedents for state support of Catholic schools also existed in America's own short history of public education. From the early part of the nineteenth century a number of communities in the East allocated public funds to Catholic schools (Gabel, 1937). New York City is a case in point. In 1822 no less than one dozen Protestant and Catholic churches received a portion of the school fund for payment of teachers' salaries (Boese, 1869, p. 102). In 1822 the Baptist Church even won the right to use any surplus of its school allotment for the construction of buildings and other purposes, though this practice ended in scandal and controversy in 1825 (Palmer, 1905, Ch. 6; Bourne, 1870, Chs. 12 & 13).

The second alternative for the nation was to establish a unified school system under secular control. This meant the elimination of religious practices offensive to any particular group. Indeed, this had been the formula that Protestants had worked out among themselves early in the nineteenth century. But now, with a large Catholic population in its midst, the nation was forced to decide whether or not to take an additional step from nondenominational to nonsectarian schools. Under this arrangement specifically Protestant practices in the schools would be eliminated and parochial schools would be denied public funds.

Of course, it was the latter option that finally became national policy. Only in retrospect, however, does it make sense to claim that the nation was committed in principle to the separation of church and state, and therefore could not subsidize parochial schools. Whatever validity this reasoning has today, it does not stand up from the vantage point of the early nineteenth century. As indicated above, before 1820 church schools were regularly supported by the state, and Catholics were sometimes given a share of the school fund. Even after the principle of nondenominationalism became established as policy, schools were pervaded by Protestant influences. The history of public education before 1850 hardly reveals a commitment to a strict separation between church and state.

Catholic appeals for a share of the school fund were finally rejected not to safeguard the principle of church-state separation, but because Americans were unwilling to support schools that were non-Protestant. It was here that the legacy of anti-Catholic bigotry and the rising tide of nativism manifested themselves in their most decisive form. The thought of financing Catholic schools was anathema to Protestants in the nineteenth century. Even if they had to give up some of their own religious prerogatives in the schools, it was a price worth paying in order to prevent the development of Popery on American soil.

More was involved than a popularly based anti-Catholicism. The nation was young and trying to forge an identity out of the mélange of ethnic and nationality groups in the population. Most leaders believed that the welfare of the nation and the future of democracy depended upon the rapid Americanization of immigrants. It was feared that a proliferation of ethnic colonies would result in independent centers of power, divided loyalties, and internal wars of the kind that ravaged Europe. Exponents of this view were found among leading educators. As one knowledgeable historian decribes Horace Mann:

Mann was tremendously impressed with the diversity of the American people. Yet he feared that conflicts of value might rip them apart and render them powerless. Dreading the destructive possibilities of religious, political, and class difference, he sought a common value system within which diversity might flourish. His quest was for a new public philosophy, a sense of community to be shared by Americans of every background and persuasion. And his instrument in this effort would be the common school (Cremin, 1961, pp. 9–10).[5]

In at least one respect enlightened and unenlightened opinion were but opposite sides of the same coin. Enlightened opinion argued the desirability of a common system of values and opted for a common school that would bring this about. Unenlightened opinion argued the undesirability of Catholic differences and the dangers of giving support to separate Catholic schools. Of course, it is not incidental that one sprung from high democratic and moral ideals, the other from vulgar bigotry. But this difference should not obscure the fact that both enlightened and unenlightened opinion were opposed to a pluralistic system of education, and questioned the viability of cultural pluralism in general.

Thus, in the final analysis it was not so much the constitutional provision for the separation of church and state as it was the unofficial commitment to a culturally integrated society that settled the school question. It was a principle of unification and homogeneity, not of separation and diversity, that proved decisive. Of course, to make the schools nonsectarian required concessions from the Protestant majority. But in granting these concessions Protestants avoided giving official sanction to the idea of a separate Catholic school system. Paradoxically, by relinquishing Protestant control of the schools, the Protestant character of the nation was preserved.

"GODLESS SCHOOLS" Once the state assumed exclusive control over public education, the ultimate elimination of religion was inevitable. If Protestants and Catholics were to be educated under one roof, the only practical solution was the secular school.

Robert Cross (1968, p. 135) points out that some liberal Catholics welcomed the establishment of free public education, despite its secular quality. They recognized that secular schools would promote economic mobility and cultural assimilation, and urged the Church to content itself with a complementary system of religious education. However, the main current of Catholic opinion, especially among the Church hierarchy, remained adamantly opposed to secular education and was determined to develop a Catholic alternative.

---

[5] From *The Transformation of the School.* Copyright © 1961 by Lawrence A. Cremin. Published by Alfred A. Knopf, Inc. Reprinted by permission.

The elimination of Protestant influences did not settle the "school question" but only transformed it. Now the issue was whether Catholics in good conscience could send their children to state schools ruled by a principle that involved the exclusion of religion. In 1891 a prominent Catholic expressed the dual nature of the Catholic dilemma with his comment that "the whole public school system is tainted with either Protestantism or irreligion" (ibid., p. 136). Catholics found themselves in a different but no less difficult bind. As one Catholic journal put it: "The more attractive and plausible State institutions are made, the greater need is there that Catholic parents keep their children away from them" (in Christ & Sherry, 1961, p. 33).

There were several related elements in the Catholic reaction to state-controlled education. One was a distrust of the state itself. In 1876 a bishop assailed the public school system as "nothing else . . . than a huge conspiracy against religion, individual liberty and enterprise, and parental rights" (Cross, 1968, p. 96). Elsewhere he wrote, "The Catholic is unwilling to transfer the responsibility of the education of his children to the state. His conscience informs him that the state is an incompetent agent to fulfill his parental duties" (McCluskey, 1964a, p. 9).

These sentiments were reiterated as recently as 1950 in a statement from the American church hierarchy. It asserted that in establishing a system of Catholic schools, "parents have acted within their competence, because it is they, and not the State, who possess the primary right to educate" ("The Child . . . ." 1950, p. 197). Antistatism on the part of the Church undoubtedly reflects the historical struggle between religious and secular authority. But there was, in fact, little in the experience of Catholics in nineteenth-century America to suggest that the state and its schools were not inimical to religion, and to Catholicism in particular.

BAPTISMAL INNOCENCE Underlying the view that the state was incompetent to educate children is a uniquely Catholic attitude concerning the moral frailties of children and the attendant responsibilities of parents and Church. In this Catholic view, children are seen as endowed with saintly innocence and moral purity. Their baptismal innocence, however, leaves them vulnerable to the influences of a decadent world, including malicious or misguided individuals who might implant children with error and vice. In the midst of this struggle between truth and error, purity and depravity, is the

Church which, through the intervention of parents, acts as spiritual benefactor, guardian of morality, and protector of young souls.

These ideas pervade the Church pronouncements on the necessity of Catholic schools that were issued periodically during the nineteenth century. A pastoral written in 1829 contained this revealing passage concerning the moral constitution of children:

... the characteristic of the child ... is the characteristic of the saint. Genuine simplicity without guile, uncalculating ardent devotion to the loving parent, preferring an humble mother in her homely garb, to a queen in her variegated decoration; exercising an irresistible power over the parental heart by the bewitching confidence of helplessness itself ("Pastoral Letter. . . ," 1829, p. 52).

The letter impressed on parents their responsibility for the spiritual development of their children and warned that failure in this regard might condemn their children to be "tortured for eternity." The road to redemption was clear: "If you would avert this dreadful calamity, attend to the education of your child."

Another pastoral in 1840 was more specific concerning the dangers of public education: "We can scarcely point out a book in general use in the ordinary schools, or even in higher seminaries, wherein covert and insidious efforts are not made to misrepresent our principles, to distort our tenets, to vilify our practices and to bring contempt upon our church and its members" ("Pastoral Letter . . . ," 1840, p. 61). At first the Church relied on these evocative tracts to convince parents to send their children to parish schools. Later moral suasion would give way to threats that absolution might be refused to parents who neglected their children's religious training.

The theme that public education endangered the souls of children was repeated with greater urgency as the century progressed. The First Plenary Council of American bishops in 1852 issued a pastoral that exhorted parents to "watch over the purity of their [children's] faith and morals with jealous vigilance" and warned of "fake and delusive theories which . . . leave youth without religion." The admonition continued:

Listen not to those who would persuade you that religion can be separated from secular instruction. If your children . . . are not taught the science of the saints, their minds will be filled with every error, and that very learning which they have acquired . . . will be an additional means of destroying the happiness of the child, embittering still more the chalice of parental disappointment, and weakening the social order ("Pastoral Letter of 1852," pp. 79–80).

Again in 1875, the theme of youthful innocence and corruptibility:

. . . children are sent to these schools from their earliest years, almost from their cradle; at which age . . . the seeds sown of virtue or of vice take fast root. To allow this tender age to pass without religion is surely a great evil . . . these schools being under no control of the Church . . . there is nothing to stop [teachers] from infusing into the young minds the seeds of error and vice ("Instruction of the Congregation . . . ," 1875, pp. 122–123).

Finally, in 1884 the Third Plenary Council formally decreed the establishment of parish schools and proclaimed that all Catholic parents were obligated to use them. The hierarchy put itself on record as believing the Church was locked in a fateful struggle "between truth and error, between Faith and Agnosticism" ("Pastoral Letter of 1884," p. 89). The outcome, it was believed, depended upon the establishment of church-controlled schools that would protect the minds and souls, the faith and morals, of Catholic children.

The Catholic belief in the moral purity of children and the importance of early religious training had deep roots in Catholic thought, dating back to the seventeenth century.[6] However, it gained new significance in the United States. The problem of being a religious minority strengthened traditional reservations concerning the encroachment of the state on religious domain. It also introduced an element of reality in Catholic fears that children would be exposed to alien ideas. Some leading Catholics believed that the very survival of Catholicism in America was at stake and that, unless children were removed from "Godless schools," church pews

---

[6] "A great change in manners took place in the course of the seventeenth century. . . . An essential concept had won acceptance: that of the innocence of childhood" (Aries, 1962, p. 110). One consequence was a corresponding emphasis on the importance of education: "The result [of the new attitude toward children] was the formation of that moral concept which insisted on the weakness of childhood rather than on . . . its 'illustrious nature,' but which associated its weakness with its innocence, the true reflection of divine purity, *and which placed education in the front rank of man's obligations"* (ibid., p. 114, italics added).

would soon be empty. This fear was expressed by one prominent bishop in a letter to the Pope in 1892:

. . . although the chief mission of the Church is to preach the Gospel of Christ, yet there is little likelihood of that Gospel reaching and abiding in the hearts of the children except through the instrumentality of the schoolhouse. . . . it will be useless to build churches that in one or two generations hence will be vacant because children or grandchildren of European parents no longer follow the religion of their ancestors. If the Church in the United States has already lost so many of her children, it is due in large degree to the want of Catholic schools (McCluskey, 1964*a*, p. 164).

Another clergyman wrote in 1907: "We will not have any educated Catholic laymen twenty years from now if non-Catholic universities are selected for the education of our Catholic youth" (in Meyer, 1907, p. 170). Such fears of cultural extinction were commonplace among immigrants, and not altogether without basis in reality, given the problems of cultural survival in a nation committed to a policy of Americanization.[7]

Virtually all Catholic leaders supported the idea of a Catholic alternative to "godless schools." However, one of the earliest dissenting voices was that of Orestes Brownson, a Protestant convert who promulgated his unorthodox views in a periodical that bore his name. Brownson argued that the minority position of Catholics made it imperative that they adapt to the dominant society and its institutions rather than withdraw into a self-imposed colony. He wrote in 1857:

When the world was Catholic . . . it was, perhaps, not unwise to bring up children in ignorance of error, and to exclude them from all intercourse or acquaintance with its adherents. . . . But in our times and country, we English-speaking Catholics are placed in a non-Catholic world, and the faithful should understand that to keep our children out of harm's way, by keeping them in ignorance of the world around them, is not practicable (*Brownson's Quarterly Review,* 1857).[8]

---

[7] Similar forebodings of religious and cultural extinction were also made about Jews. For example, one sociologist warned in 1935 that the paucity of children receiving religious education "might cause the total eclipse of the Jewish church in the United States" (Engleman, 1921, p. 51). Of course, for both Catholics and Jews such dire warnings prompted the development of religious schools that prevented the most pessimistic predictions from being realized.

[8] In Frank L. Christ and Gerard E. Sherry (eds.), *American Catholicism and the Intellectual Ideal* (p. 18). Copyright © 1961 by Appleton-Century-Crofts, Inc. Reprinted by permission of the publisher.

Although not opposed to religious education, Brownson advised Catholics not to exaggerate the defects of the public school. He further cautioned against discouraging free inquiry and a creative spirit. To place restrictions on literature and science, he wrote, "tends only to drive from our ranks a large proportion of those who by their natural talents are best fitted to extend and adorn Catholic literature and science." These were views that would win increasing acceptance among Catholic intellectuals over the next century.

So far this chapter has analyzed five factors that entered into Catholic antagonism toward public education: (1) a response to the dilemma of being a minority religion in a nation where anti-Catholicism ran high; (2) a desire on the part of immigrants to protect their children from the assimilating influences of the public schools; (3) a reaction against the content of public education—that is, its suffusion first with Protestantism and later with secularism; (4) a traditional distrust of the state that was reinforced in America; (5) a fear, partly based on a conception of the baptismal innocence of children, that their faith and morals would be undermined in the public schools. These factors are interrelated and mutually reinforcing. No one of them constitutes an adequate explanation of why American Catholicism channeled its limited resources into an extensive system of parish schools, but collectively they produced this result.

One other factor requires attention: the Catholic concept of education differed in important respects from the pedagogical philosophy guiding public education. Not only did this provide another inducement to build parochial schools, but it also determined the nature of the education that Catholic children received in those schools.

A "CATHOLIC EDUCATION"   The Second Plenary Council declared: "To develop the intellect and store it with knowledge, while the heart and its affections are left without the control of the religious principle, sustained by religious practices, is to mistake the nature and object of education" ("Pastoral Letter of 1866," p. 83). The hallmark of a Catholic education was that religious principles were infused throughout the educational process. Catholics believed in the unity of the intellectual, moral, and physical development of children, and on this ground could not accept the distinction between secular and religious training.

American public education has always counted moral education among its educational priorities, and this has nearly always meant Christian morality. But since the mid-nineteenth century the trend has been to remove education from an explicitly religious context. For Catholics, however, the goals of moral education and of religious training were inseparable. In the traditional Catholic view there is no basis for moral authority other than religion. This was clearly spelled out in the pastoral from the Third Plenary Council in 1884: "Take away religion from a people, and morality will soon follow; morality gone, even their physical condition will ere long degenerate into corruption which breeds decrepitude, while their intellectual attainments would only serve as a light to guide them to deeper depths of vice and ruin" ("Pastoral Letter of 1884," p. 90). Here lies the strain of anti-intellectualism in traditional Catholic thought: without the constraining influence of religion, knowledge itself was viewed as a danger, leading to "deeper depths of vice and ruin."

Just as Catholics opposed the separation of religion from moral education, they opposed its separation from vocational training. In the Catholic *Weltanschauung* religious values ought to pervade all forms of human activity. Catholics were skeptical of the heavy emphasis in the public schools on the preparation of children for adult vocations. Divorced from religion, Catholics believed, vocational training would result in the exclusion of religious and ethical values from commercial and other vocational activities. This belief was also expressed in the pastoral of the Third Plenary Council:

To shut religion out of the school, and keep it for home and the Church, is, logically, to train up a generation that will consider religion good for the home and the Church, but not for the practical business of real life. But a more fake and pernicious notion could not be imagined. Religion, in order to elevate a people, should inspire their whole life and rule their relation with one another ("Pastoral Letter of 1884," p. 91).

This refusal to separate the secular from the religious provided the rationale for full-time Catholic schools. To limit religious training to Sunday or afternoon schools seemed tantamount to saying that religious values were irrelevant to the rest of life's activities.

More was involved than this, however. For Catholics, the real consequence of irreligion was not secularism but materialism. There was abundant evidence in late nineteenth-century America that in their pursuit of money, power, and wordly success, people tended to abandon moral standards and restraints. "A civilization without religion," warned the Third Plenary Council, "would be a civilization of 'the struggle for existence, and the survival of the fittest,' in which cunning and strength would become the substitutes for principle, virtue, conscience and duty" ("Pastoral Letter of 1884," p. 90).

In the Catholic view, the purpose of education was to cultivate moral virtue and pursue religious truths. Given these attitudes, it is not surprising that Catholics were strongly committed to a classical education. Studies in the humanities, classics, and philosophy were viewed as bringing students closer to God and therefore consistent with the Church's educational ideals. In contrast, science and vocational training seemed spiritually vacant, and came dangerously close to substituting a base materialism for high moral purpose.

More than the secular institutions, Catholic intellectuals and colleges resisted the trend at the end of the nineteenth century to incorporate science and vocational training into the regular college curriculum. They were confident that this was not only in their religious interests, but also required to preserve high standards of scholarship. In 1904 one Catholic speaker could exult over the superiority of Catholic colleges:

It has also been proved beyond all doubt that our Catholic colleges (at least the standard ones) are superior in genuine scholarship to the great Protestant and secular universities. They require higher standards for admission and graduation. A student may be admitted to Harvard University or Columbia College today without any knowledge of Latin or Greek, and may then choose his own subjects for bachelor's degree with such discretion as to relieve him almost entirely from any serious studies, while the Catholic colleges almost universally insist on the study of the classical languages, and in addition to Science and Literature, on a solid course of Philosophy (Conway, 1904).[9]

This confidence was short-lived, however. In clinging to a classical program, Catholic institutions were going against major educational trends, and the costs soon became apparent. In the 1920s wide publicity was given to a study reporting that Catholics were grossly underrepresented among prominent Americans listed in *Who's*

[9] From *The Catholic Mind.* Reprinted by permission of America Press. Copyright © 1904. All rights reserved. (America Press, Inc., 106 W. 56th St., New York, N.Y. 10019)

Who in America (Huntington & Whitney, 1927). Another survey of scientists published in the 1927 edition of *American Men of Science* yielded the same result (Lehman & Witty, 1931). So have more recent investigations, most notably Knapp and Goodrich's 1952 study of *Origins of American Scientists* (Knapp & Goodrich, 1952; Knapp & Greenbaum, 1953).

These studies stimulated and have helped to sustain a mood of self-examination and criticism within the Church. Battlelines were drawn along the usual conservative-liberal dimension. Conservatives were unmoved by statistical findings showing an underproduction of scientists. Firmly committed to a classical education, they had no desire to emulate the secular university. Liberals did not deny the special functions of the Catholic college, but argued that they should be expanded to include disciplines and modes of scholarship that were gaining acceptance in the secular university. Otherwise, they warned, Catholic colleges would be denied academic respectability and left out of the important intellectual currents of the age. One liberal wrote in 1939:

> It is obvious that all Catholic universities worthy of the name should consider teaching and research their basic function, whatever other functions according to special conditions they may be expected to perform. Catholic universities must put far more emphasis on research and scholarly publication. Our record of productive scholarship in all but a few fields is still a pitiful one. Yet we shall never win respect for the Church and her teachings among non-Catholic intellectuals . . . until we have convinced them by scholarship of high order that we can be good scholars and remain staunch Catholics (McGuire, 1939).[10]

He urged Catholic colleges to undertake a program of research in the natural and social sciences.

This, conservatives believed, was not simply undesirable, but antithetical to the purpose and function of a Catholic university. A conservative wrote in 1938: "It is frequently said and almost universally assumed that the function of the graduate school is research. But . . . such a view is in conflict with the whole Catholic tradition of education and . . . a Catholic university which accepts research as the dominant objective of its graduate school, is by that much attempting the impossible task of being Catholic in creed and

[10] In Frank L. Christ and Gerard E. Sherry (eds.), *American Catholicism and the Intellectual Ideal* (p. 120). Copyright © 1961 by Appleton-Century-Crofts, Inc. Reprinted by permission of the publisher.

anti-Catholic in culture" (Bull, 1938, pp. 112–113). This writer believed that research was "at war with the whole Catholic life of the mind" (ibid., p. 115). He pointed to a number of antinomies that differentiate research from the "Catholic life of the mind: organic unity of knowledge vs. disintegration; humanism vs. dehumanization; the sense of tradition and of wisdom achieved vs. 'progress': of principles vs. fact; of contemplation vs. 'research'" (Bull, 1938, p. 114).

Catholic thought had been laden with a number of other dichotomies: truth and error, virtue and vice, religion and atheism, spiritualism and materialism, the survival or dissolution of the Church. These distinctions expressed themselves in the battle against public education, and provided an ideological framework for establishing a system of education under Catholic control. Finally, the Catholic *Weltanschauung* determined the character of Catholic education. In aim as well as substance, it differed fundamentally from the educational program in the public schools. However, the Catholic commitment to a classical education, although consistent with the pedagogy of secular institutions for most of the nineteenth century, became increasingly anachronistic in the twentieth century. It was inevitable that Catholic institutions would not produce the kind of scholars and scientists that measured up to prevailing standards and were rewarded by being listed in *Who's Who in America.*

CONCLUSION In the past half-century American Catholicism has undergone drastic change in its relation to the larger society. The shock waves that both Protestants and Catholics experienced as a result of Catholic immigration have long since passed, and while Protestant-Catholic conflict still exists, it is at minimal levels. Most of the conditions that triggered the Catholic reaction against public schools and secular education have disappeared or lost their force. The absorption of the nation's white minorities into the cultural mainstream has all but eliminated the ethnic factor in Catholic attitudes toward education. In this process Catholics have accommodated themselves to the secular currents in American society. Few Catholics, including those who enroll their children in parochial schools, believe that the souls of their children are endangered by public education. Of course, controversy over state support of parochial education continues, but the conflict has been contained within established political structures and is no longer a source of deep division. Finally, parochial education has itself undergone considerable reform, partly in response to past failures. Today the educational program of Catholic schools is in most respects comparable to that of public schools, both in quality and content. A recent study (Greeley & Rossi, 1966) found almost no differences between parochial and public school children in terms of their adult careers, their social attitudes, or even their religious behavior.

The weight of historical evidence suggests that Catholic problems with American educational institutions were not expressions of a native anti-intellectualism emanating from Catholic religion, but rather were the result of social conditions in nineteenth-century America. If this proposition is correct, then we should be witnessing a gradual increase in Catholic representation among the nation's scholars and scientists. This indeed is the case, as is demonstrated in Part III of this study.

Part Two
Theories of Religion and Intellectual Achievement

It is clear from the analysis of Part 1 that even before their arrival in America, Jews and Catholics differed in their cultural orientations toward education. Indeed, these cultural differences are generally assumed to be the principal reason that Jews historically have been overrepresented, and Catholics underrepresented, in the ranks of the nation's scholars and scientists. Chapter 3 examines the ethnographic and historical evidence that has been used as the basis for cultural interpretations of Jewish-Catholic differences in intellectual achievement. Chapter 4 then explores differences between Jewish and Catholic immigrants along several dimensions of social class. This raises the most important theoretical problem of this study: To what extent are Jewish-Catholic differences in intellectual achievement a product of the cultural baggage that each group carried with it to America? And to what extent did these different cultural orientations merely reflect differences in underlying social class factors?

3. Cultural Differences between Jewish and Catholic Immigrants

Since Weber's classic study of *The Protestant Ethic and the Spirit of Capitalism* a plethora of studies have examined the relationship between religious background and worldly success.[1] Invariably, Jews are found to rank higher than Catholics in terms of class position and intellectual achievement and, almost invariably, cultural theories are advanced to explain these differences. These theories are basically of two kinds. The first belongs to an anthropological tradition in that its explanatory focus is on the configuration of values and attitudes of the religious group. Specifically, it looks for areas of compatibility or incompatibility between the value system of the religious group and the value system of the secular society. In the case of Jews, it is suggested, there was a high degree of correspondence or adaptability between religious values and the values associated with modern industrial society. In the case of Catholics, certain disparities and incongruities between religious and secular values are said to be the reason for their lower rate of worldly success.

A second theoretical tradition has been developed by social psychologists. These theories also focus on the surface values of religious groups, but they go on to explore the processes whereby these cultural trends become significant for individual behavior. Essentially they deal with the psychological dimensions of value systems, and the ways in which cultural values are integrated into personality structure. Let us examine each of these theoretical traditions in greater detail.

---

[1] For a survey of research on the relationship between religion and social class, see Warren (1970); and Rhodes and Nam (1970).

"Jewish intellectualism"

The notion that the high Jewish representation among scholars, scientists, and intellectuals is an outgrowth of Jewish scholarly traditions is virtually an article of faith in the social sciences. It has entered into the work of almost anyone who has written on this subject, including Louis Wirth, Talcott Parsons, Will Herberg, Nathan Glazer, and numerous others.[2] The argument is most fully developed and documented in a study by Mark Zborowski and Elizabeth Herzog entitled *Life Is with People* (1962).

Zborowski and Herzog, both anthropologists, sought to re-create the social and cultural life of the *shtetl,* the small Jewish settlement of Eastern Europe. Their chief source of data came from lengthy interviews with over a hundred immigrant Jews, supplemented by miscellaneous life histories and literary materials. Although their book has been criticized for presenting a romantic and idealized account of Jewish cultural origins, nevertheless it has achieved wide acceptance among social scientists. Undoubtedly it is the study most often cited in support of the thesis that Jewish intellectual achievement is a product of a reverence for learning deeply embedded in Jewish culture and history.

According to Zborowski and Herzog, Jewish learned traditions have developed over two millenia of time, and were preserved in the shtetl where scholarship "remained the dominant force of the culture" (Zborowski & Herzog, 1962, p. 104). They write:

> Not every Jew in the shtetl is a scholar or even a learned man, but *intellectual achievement is the universally accepted goal.* There are few Jews from Eastern Europe who have not attended the kheder at least for a short time. . . . And the traditional expectation for a boy born in the shtetl is that from the kheder to the grave he will devote some portion of his time to study (ibid., p. 102, italics added).

For shtetl Jews, scholarship was a moral imperative just as work was for seventeenth-century Puritans. Scholars were accorded special prestige and authority in the Jewish community. And parents encouraged and exulted in the scholastic achievements of their (male) children. Both as an ethos and an activity, book learning was so much a part of everyday routine that, according to Zborow-

---

[2] The "scholarship theory" of Jewish mobility, as it appears in the works of these sociologists, is briefly reviewed by Slater (1969).

ski and Herzog, "from the kheder to the grave" Jews were surrounded by a "cult of scholarship."

More than a religious imperative and a cultural value, learning was embedded in social institutions. Formal education typically began between the ages of three and five, and the school day stretched from 8 A.M. until 6 P.M. except on the Sabbath. At first teaching consisted of repetitious and mechanical learning, but in later years Talmudic study became intellectually challenging. Solving a Talmudic question demanded "penetration, scholarship, imagination, memory, logic, wit, subtlety" (ibid., p. 98). Furthermore, it had its own style of argument involving "comparison of different interpretations, analysis of all possible and impossible aspects of a given problem, and—through an ingenious intellectual combination—the final solution to an apparently insoluble problem (ibid.). This dialectical mode of argument, some writers have suggested, is the source of a unique intellectual style often found among Jewish scholars and intellectuals.

In a recent article one sociologist—Miriam Slater—attempts to refute the "scholarship theory" of Jewish success. Slater argues that Jewish intellectual tradition "was not likely to be continuous with American educational institutions." On the contrary, in style, content, and purpose, Jewish scholarship was completely at odds with modern secular education. Thus, far from being an asset, "insofar as such [shtetl] goals were internalized we should expect them to be a deterrent to desiring higher education" (Slater, 1969, p. 372). Slater's conclusion is that Jewish class mobility is a product not of Jewish intellectual traditions but of certain "middle-class orientations," especially a striving for material success.

Slater is undoubtedly correct that there was little in the content of Talmudic scholarship that provided direct continuities with modern educational systems. As Lewis Feuer (1963, p. 303) points out, "this sterile type of [Talmudic] 'learning' and disputation was an obstacle to the development of science among the Jews, a hurdle they had to surmount." Like Catholic scholasticism and Protestant fundamentalism, the Talmudic tradition was hostile to science. Frequently, orthodox Jews, like their Christian counterparts, strenuously resisted secular education.

Nevertheless, Slater overlooks other more subtle ways in which Jewish intellectual traditions promoted educational achievement and class mobility among immigrant Jews. The continuity was not one of content, but of style; not of substance, but of orientation. Even Zborowski does not claim that Talmudic scholarship in and of itself was an educational asset for Eastern European immigrants. Rather he suggests that Jewish intellectual traditions facilitated the *transition* from an archaic system of religious instruction to modern secular education: "In the United States, parents do not necessarily save their money in order to send their children to the kheder or the yeshiva, but they may struggle and sacrifice in order to provide a college or university education. The professional man . . . takes the place of the talmud kholshom as the ideal son or son-in-law" (Zborowski, 1955, p. 139).[3] As this passage implies, Zborowski agrees with Slater that Jews were driven by a desire for economic gain and social advancement. But he sees economic motives and attitudes toward education as complementary and mutually reinforcing. The significance of outdated intellectual traditions is that, once adapted to the American situation, they facilitated class mobility through American educational institutions.

In addition, given the religious symbolism traditionally connected with study, the process of mobility through education became endowed with quasi-religious significance. That is to say, educational values gave moral legitimacy to occupational mobility and the accumulation of wealth. As Zborowski (1955, p. 140) comments: "In the United States intellectual activity is used to enable one to earn money in an honorific way—a way that itself is a badge of academic accomplishment." The Jewish scholar who eschewed commercial activity was replaced as a cultural model by the secular Jew, most clearly personified by the Jewish doctor, whose education became the source of wealth and status.

This cultural metamorphosis is vividly illustrated by the main character in Abraham Cahan's novel, *The Rise of David Levinsky,* first published in 1917. Once a Talmudic scholar in Russia, David Levinsky immigrates to America and makes a fortune in the garment industry. He is troubled, however, by the fact that he never realized his ambition to go to college (his success lacked moral legitimacy). He remembers as a youth gazing at the "humble spires" of City College, and thinks to himself: "My old religion had gradually fallen to pieces, and if its place was taken by something else, . . . that something was the red, church-like structure on the southeast

[3] In Margaret Mead and Martha Wolfenstein (eds.), *Childhood in Contemporary Cultures.* Copyright © 1955 by the University of Chicago. All rights reserved. Reprinted by permission of the publisher.

corner of Lexington Avenue and Twenty-Third Street. It was the synagogue of my second life" (Cahan, 1960, p. 169). "The synagogue of my second life" epitomizes the transfer of religious symbolism from religious to secular education and the attendant sanctification of scholarly life. As Levinsky says of City College:

It was not merely a place in which I was to fit myself for the battle of life, not merely one in which I was going to acquire knowledge. It was a symbol of spiritual promotion as well. University-bred people were the real nobility of the world. A college diploma was a certificate of moral as well as intellectual aristocracy (ibid.).

"Catholic Anti-intellectualism"[4]

Whereas the great majority of American Jews have their origins in Eastern Europe, the national background of American Catholics is much more varied. Italy, Ireland, Germany, France, Poland, Eastern Europe, Spain, and Latin America have all contributed substantially to the nation's Catholic population. Inasmuch as the character of Catholicism varies from one country to the next, generalization is hazardous at best. The ensuing discussion focuses exclusively on Italian Catholics. Not only do Italians constitute the largest ethnic bloc within the Catholic population, but the cultural background of Italian immigrants provides the sharpest contrast with Jewish immigrants who arrived at approximately the same point in time.

    One of the most valuable ethnographic accounts of the cultural

---

[4] In his essay entitled "Reflections on Anti-Intellectualism," Morton White draws a distinction between anti-intellectuals and anti-intellectualists. The anti-intellectual is "one who is hostile to intellectuals." He is "usually an ordinary man, *non*-intellectual, to whom an egg-head is an egg-head, whether scientist, historian or philosopher, rationalist or empiricist, hard-boiled or scrambled. . . . The important contrast is that between the pursuits of the professor, artist, scholar, and scientist, on the one hand, and those of the business man, plumber, secretary, barber, and politician, on the other." In contrast, the anti-intellectualist is one who is hostile to the philosophical doctrine known as intellectualism. . . . Unlike the anti-intellectual, the anti-intellectualist may press the claims of the heart and the hand against those of the head, or he may think of intuition as a superior faculty to be distinguished sharply from that employed by the mathematician or the experimental scientist" (White, 1962, p. 457).

    While Chapter 2 dealt with anti-intellectualism of this second type, the present chapter deals with the first type—that is, anti-intellectualism in the sense of a hostility to intellectuals or their activities, and a disregard for formal learning.

origins of Italian immigrants is found in a book by Leonard Covello on *The Social Background of the Italo-American School Child* (1967). Originally written as a doctoral dissertation at New York University in 1944, the book was based on research conducted over a ten-year period in both Italy and the United States. During this time Covello was a teacher and administrator in the Italian community of East Harlem in New York City. His study was an attempt to shed light on the educational problems of Italian-American schoolchildren. These problems manifested themselves in "truancy, absence, cutting classes, lateness, and disciplinary problems" (Covello, 1967, p. 185),[5] all of which were far more prevalent among high school students of Italian origin than among the general school population. Still more important, Italian children left school at an earlier age than others. Thanks probably to his Italian background, Covello steered clear of the Darwinian theories that were commonly invoked to explain the social problems of immigrants from Southern Europe. Instead he viewed the educational problems of second-generation Italians as an outgrowth of the Southern Italian peasant society from which their parents came.

When the political unification of Italy was achieved in 1870, economically and culturally Italy was still a divided country. Indeed, as the North underwent the process of industrial development and urbanization, the disparities between the North and the South became even wider. The peasant economy of southern Italy remained essentially unchanged from its century-old cast. The population consisted mostly of propertyless peasants called *contadinos* who worked as agricultural laborers under an exploitative system of contract labor. The economic and social inequalities between the North and South were reflected in popular attitudes, and the South was generally regarded as a culturally backward and semi-barbaric region cut off from the body politic. Economically it functioned as an agricultural colony, providing the necessary agricultural surplus for the industrial North.

The North, furthermore, dominated the nation's political institutions and the instruments of government were invariably used to the detriment of the South. In education this took the form of grossly unequal expenditures of school funds. According to one report, between 1900 and 1910 the central government allocated 5 lire per inhabitant of northern Italy but only 1.8 lire per inhabitant

[5] Copyright © 1967, 1972 by Francesco Cordasco. All quotations from Covello reprinted by permission of F. Cordasco.

of the South. Schools in the South were few, poorly equipped, and often inaccessible. The compulsory school attendance law, passed in 1877, was rarely enforced. As a consequence, while the rates of illiteracy in the North steadily declined, almost no progress was made in the South. In 1901, the peak period of Italian immigration to America, the rate of illiteracy in most southern provinces exceeded 70 percent. As late as 1913, illiteracy was still universal in some villages (ibid., pp. 244–247).

The fact that authority over the schools derived from the North also was significant for the kind of education received in southern schools. As Covello writes: "The philosophy underlying the function and activity of the school in southern Italy was based . . . on cultural norms of northern Italy" (ibid., p. 254). In the first place, problems arose with language, since vernaculars and dialects varied from province to province and even among towns within a province. Also, teachers rarely spoke in the local idiom. Covello observed that the use of literary Italian in the schools "was a source of frequent irritation to parents" (ibid., p. 264), and proved unmanageable for most children. From the vantage point of the southern Italian peasant, the schools represented an alien culture. Ironically, the pariah status of Jews in Eastern Europe gave them a greater measure of control over their educational institutions.

In addition, the highly organized formal education of the schools clashed fundamentally with southern Italian values. As in every folk society, knowledge consisted of the accumulated experience of past generations and an elaborate system of moral codes: "well-defined notions concerning treatment of parents, relatives, attitudes toward women, strangers, proper food, ways of dealing with evil spirits, prayers—all forms of group thinking and group behavior were the content of education" (ibid., p. 266). Transmission of this culture occurred primarily through the family and with the benefit of a rich folklore. Given the extraordinary emphasis on family values, the school came to be viewed as a threat to the integrity and strength of the family itself. Unlike shtetl Jews, Italian children received little encouragement from their parents insofar as schooling was concerned; indeed, their parents often conspired to circumvent the compulsory school law, especially during periods when their children's labor was needed in the fields.

It would be erroneous, however, to conclude that education per se received low priority in the value system. Rather, as Covello observed, "to the Italian parent, the idea of education or his concept of a person *buon educato* was remote from the concepts which served as a basis of school education" (ibid., p. 254). This southern Italian expression, *buon educato,* is the key to understanding the peasant attitude toward education. *Buon educato* was "an indication of having absorbed the codes of etiquette, manners, and behavior norms that were appropriate and proper for all occasion in the familial or communal life." In contrast, *mal educato* was a term of reproach and a slur against the individual and family that did not behave according to existing mores (ibid., p. 261).

Even the common language drew a sharp distinction between *educato* and *istruito: "Una persona educata* is a respectful, well-mannered person. *Una persona istruita* is a learned person; one who has been instructed in the schools—has school learning. A person may be *ben istruito* (well instructed) but *mal educato* (badly mannered). The southern Italian attaches the greatest importance to a person being *buon educato* rather than *istruito"* (ibid., p. 254). Formal education was resisted not only because it neglected moral education for the sake of book learning, but also because it subverted traditional codes of behavior. Thus, opposition to teaching girls to read and write was based on a fear that such girls might be tempted to write letters to their suitors. Similarly, it was feared that boys would be lured away from traditional occupations. The most serious danger, however, was that schooling might undermine family values. One of Covello's informants described his father's disdain for American education in these terms: "What good is it if a boy is bright and intelligent in school, and then does not know enough to respect his family? Such a boy would be worth nothing" (ibid., p. 261).

In the peasant's scheme of things, education should be practical. Above all, it should prepare the child for a life of adversity.

In preparation for the hard, crude existence of the *contadino* in his struggle for bare existence, certain qualities were ruthlessly inculcated: early rising, extremely long hours of hard work, disregard for the summer heat or the bitter cold of winter, extreme unconcern for personal appearance while at work or for personal hygiene, simple food with little variety; and only extreme illness was an excuse to get a respite from work. Knowledge of how to protect oneself against man and beast was inculcated at an early age (ibid., p. 270).

What is the purpose of cultivating the mind when one is confronted with a struggle for survival? Underlying southern Italian attitudes toward education was the realization that their life chances were severely limited and that their children would certainly be peasants.

Covello was sensitive to the existential basis for the southern Italian's disregard for education:

As a peasant, unable to perceive things *in abstracto,* and as a man of the soil, he perceived education in association with material benefits. He saw the need to educate his children only in so far as the school provided means for bettering one's economic condition, or for breaking through the caste system. But since few precedents existed where a peasant's son became anything else but a peasant, the *contadino* almost never entertained the possibility of his son's becoming a doctor, a lawyer, or embarking on some other professional career (ibid., p. 256).

No peasant society is likely to see the worth of intellectual abstractions or to value education for its own sake. The fact of the matter is that the *contadino's* attitudes toward education were remarkably adapted to his real life situation. To quote Covello once again: "The informal education of the child had all the elements of an all-round, all-inclusive education to meet all possible situations that were present within the confines of the isolated villages of southern Italy. *The education was narrow, limited, even primitive, but definitely functional"* (ibid., p. 266, italics added). Conversely, to encourage schooling and to value learning would have been impossibly discrepant with the *contadino's* life situation and dysfunctional for individual and collective survival. In the incontrovertible logic of one Italian peasant: "If our children don't go to school, no harm results. But if the sheep don't eat, they will die. The school can wait but not our sheep" (ibid., p. 257).

Covello's study provides many dramatic contrasts between southern Italians and shtetl Jews. But nowhere is the contrast more striking than in the relation of religious institutions to education. According to Covello, the educational functions of the Church were practically nil:

If one were to discount the occasions when priests were employed as teachers, the educational influences of the Church and the priest were hardly worth mentioning. Even in the field of religious training their influence was negligible. With no religious training in schools at all, the only religious instruction was given in a catechism class in preparation for the confirmation period of the child (ibid., p. 139).

Of the many factors that explain the indifference of the Church with respect to education, two stand out. In the first place, priests belonged to the privileged class and shared its prejudices toward popular education, especially when it came to southerners. Secondly, during the late nineteenth century the government took steps to eliminate religion from state schools. The Church afterwards lost interest in the schools, and even viewed them as a threat to the simple faith and passivity of the Italian peasantry. According to one source:

> . . . the church is adverse that its adherents shall conform to the law which says that every Italian child shall attend school for a certain number of years. Their reason . . . is that such education is devoid of any religious character, and in reality tends, occultly or openly, to teach that which is subversive of the church's authority (Williams, 1938, p. 127).

In some countries the Church took an active interest in education because it wanted its parishioners to be able to read the Bible. However, in southern Italy, "the reading of the prayer book was neither necessary, desirable, nor encouraged by the church" (ibid., p. 258). The Church was not the most important source of southern Italian attitudes to education, but it did give them religious and moral sanction.

SOCIAL-PSYCHOLOGI-CAL THEORIES OF ACHIEVEMENT
The anthropological studies just examined point up the many ways in which Russian Jews and southern Italians differed in their intellectual traditions and their attitudes toward education. Psychological studies on this subject usually accept these cultural differences as givens. The questions they raise concern the transmission of these values within the context of the family. The most influential of these studies, judging from the frequent citations to it and its republication in several collections, is Fred Strodtbeck's monograph on "Family Interaction, Values, and Achievement."[6]

Strodtbeck sets out to explain why Jews in America have had a higher rate of class mobility than Italians. Although conceding that the two groups have different attitudes and values with respect to education, he asserts that "this is a minor difference . . . all families in our culture tend to see the school system as a means of improving their position in the status structure" (Strodtbeck, 1958, pp. 146–147). He then proceeds to look for the sources of differential achievement in patterns of family interaction, on the assumption that adjustments to authority relationships within the family are related to performance in the larger social system.

---

[6] Strodtbeck (1958). Other examples of studies of religion and achievement from a social-psychological perspective are Veroff and Feld (1962); Kohn and Schooler (1969); and Rosen (1959).

Although Strodtbeck employed a variety of research methods, his most important findings were based on questionnaires administered to high school students in public and parochial schools in New Haven, Connecticut. From an original set of 15 measures of achievement potential Strodtbeck found that 6 correlated with actual achievement and also discriminated between Jewish and Italian students. On the basis of a factor analysis, he classified these 6 items into 3 sets of value orientations (ibid., p. 169).

	Percentage agree	
	Jews	*Italians*
(1) A belief that the world is orderly and amenable to rational mastery, as opposed to a belief in destiny and the futility of planning for the future:		
Planning only makes a person unhappy since your plans hardly ever work out anyway.	10	38
When a man is born, the success he's going to have is already in the cards, so he might as well accept it and not fight against it.	2	25
(2) A willingness to leave home to make one's way in life:		
Even when teen-agers get married, their main loyalty still belongs to their fathers and mothers.	36	54
When the time comes for a boy to take a job, he should stay near his parents, even if it means giving up a good job opportunity.	9	18
Nothing in life is worth the sacrifice of moving away from your parents.	18	41
(3) A preference for individual rather than collective credit for work done:		
The best kind of job to have is one where you are part of an organization all working together even if you don't get individual credit.	46	72

These comparisons indicate substantial differences between Jews and Italians in attitudes that predict actual achievement. The important question, however, is not whether these differences exist, but what their sources are.

By implication, Strodtbeck denies that these value orientations are aspects of culture in the anthropological sense — that is, passed on from one generation to the next through the socialization process. Instead he interprets them as products of a particular form of family interaction where power is shared equally between the father and the mother. His basic assumption is that "this power balance in the family is of importance in giving a child ideas that will bear on his later success or failure" (ibid., p. 189). In a democratic family situation, according to Strodtbeck, the child will develop a sense of his own competence, and, having adjusted to power relationships within the family, he easily generalizes this experience to the outside world and is spurred on to higher levels of achievement.

Strodtbeck's data show that in father-dominated families both the mother and son score lower on measures of achievement potential: " . . . the less the mother and son are dominated by the father in the power area, the greater the disposition of both to believe that the world can be rationally mastered and that a son should risk separation from his parents" (ibid., p. 183). His data also indicate that, in comparison to Italians, Jewish families tend to be more egalitarian. Unfortunately, Strodtbeck does not control for ethnic background when reporting the relationship between family interaction patterns and achievement potential. If his reasoning is correct, the difference between Jews and Italians in achievement potential should be sharply reduced among those with similar patterns of family interaction. However, it is possible that Jewish children score high on achievement orientation, and Italian children low, no matter what the power balance in the family. Without this empirical test, Strodtbeck has not demonstrated the major claim of his paper: that it is the democratic character of the Jewish family that produces highly motivated and achieving children.

There is a still more serious flaw in Strodtbeck's thesis, one that he acknowledges but nevertheless minimizes. His analysis showed that differences in the achievement orientations of Jewish and Italian students disappeared once the social class level of their fathers was controlled (ibid., p. 173). In other words, the lower achievement orientation of Italian children is the result of their having fathers whose achievement level is relatively low. Conversely, the higher achievement scores of Jewish children reflect the higher class position of their parents.

It is possible, even likely, that ethnic factors operated to determine the achievement levels of the fathers. Nevertheless, there is apparently no residual or persistent effect of ethnic background independent of social class when it comes to the next generation. As Strodtbeck himself observed, " . . . whatever differences in values and family interaction originally existed, they are disappearing as both groups [Italians and Jews] are assimilated into American life" (ibid., p. 185). The overall implication is that ethnic factors may have influenced the initial adjustment of Jewish and Italian immigrants, but after this initial phase social class factors tend to override ethnicity as determinants of attitudes and mobility patterns in successive generations.

Another psychocultural interpretation of religious differences in achievement is found in Bernard Rosen's paper, "Race, Ethnicity, and the Achievement Syndrome" (1959). In the tradition of McClelland and Strodtbeck, Rosen conceives of the achievement syndrome as having three constituent elements: achievement motivation, value orientations, and educational-vocational aspirations. Of the three, achievement motivation is the most basic. It refers to "the internal impetus to excel" that, according to Rosen, is developed in early childhood. This psychological urge is later given content and direction by the cultural values acquired at more advanced stages of the child's development. In contrast to these cultural values, however, achievement motivation has distinctive psychodynamic sources related to the childrearing practices of different ethnic groups. While Rosen does not have original data to prove his case, his reading of ethnographic studies led him to conclude that "Protestants, Jews, and Greeks place a greater emphasis on independence and achievement training than southern Italians and French-Canadians" (Rosen, 1959, p. 52).

This last assumption is open to serious question. Covello observed that the pressures of survival in the world of southern Italian peasants required that children be introduced into adult responsibilities at a very early age. As he writes: "The prolonged period of social infancy characteristic of a formal society, where it extends through physical adolescence and even through the youth period, was entirely absent and the concept was alien and antagonistic to the southern Italian contadino" (Covello, 1967, p. 265). If anything, this early "independence training" obstructed rather than facilitated academic achievement, which necessarily depends upon an extended period of child socialization. Covello's observations are consistent with the research conducted by Oscar Lewis which shows that an adumbrated childhood is generally characteristic of groups living under conditions of extreme poverty (Lewis, 1968, p. xvii). Indeed, when Rosen briefly considers the case of American Negroes, he is forced to concede that black children typically receive early training in self-reliance. "But," he adds, "there is little evidence of much stress upon achievement training" (Rosen, 1959, p. 52).

What, then, is left of Rosen's thesis concerning the effect of child-rearing practices on adult achievement? Stripped of its assumptions regarding independence training, one is left with the unsurprising finding that achieving parents produce achieving children. As in the Strodtbeck study, when Rosen controlled for the social class of parents, he found that differences in achievement between ethnic groups were sharply reduced.[7] There is little evidence in either study that patterns of family interaction—power relationships or specific childrearing practices—explain ethnic differences in achievement.[8]

The main value of the psychologically oriented studies is that they spell out the psychological dimensions and correlates of achievement. The elements they identify—a sense of mastery over one's environment, independence from family and other primary groups, pride in individual accomplishment, an ability to defer gratification, a need to excel, a competitive spirit, high aspirational levels, etc.—all constitute a description of the psychological and attitudinal

[7] Other empirical studies of the relation between religion and socioeconomic achievement also report that religious differences are substantially reduced once social class background is controlled. For example, one study (Mack, Murphy, & Yellin, 1956) found no differences in mobility patterns between Protestants and Catholics in three specific occupations. Another study concluded that "once equated with respect to starting point in the social structure and educational attainment, the occupational achievement of one national-origin group differs little from that of another" (Duncan, 1968, p. 356). A third study found that once place of residence and education were controlled, "there is a considerable narrowing of the differentials in socioeconomic status among the three religious groups" (Goldstein, 1969, p. 612).

Although studies commonly find that religion has some remaining influence after social class is controlled, from a theoretical standpoint this is less important than the fact that the relationship between religion and achievement is substantially reduced. Due to inaccurate measurement and other technical factors there is always bound to be some residual variation, and it is rare for statistical relationships to vanish completely when test factors are introduced.

[8] This is not to say that such factors as family interaction or childrearing practices are irrelevant to adult achievement. On the contrary, the family is obviously the locus where many of the capacities for achievement are acquired. However, there is much evidence to suggest that, at least in contemporary American society, these socialization patterns are far more influenced by social class than by ethnicity as such.

concomitants of achievement. But in no way do they constitute an explanation. This is the reason the statistical relationship between ethnicity and achievement tends to vanish once social class is controlled: persons who achieve or who come from achieving backgrounds invariably exhibit the "achievement syndrome," whereas those who are not achievers almost by definition lack achievement qualities (unless encumbered by external obstacles such as racial discrimination). To explain the higher rate of Jewish achievement by the fact that Jews more often possess the achievement syndrome is to explain nothing at all. The crucial question remains: *why* do Jews more often have the attitudes and psychology that promote achievement and class mobility? In the final analysis, the psychologically oriented theories enrich our descriptive understanding of the psychological dimensions of achievement, but they lack explanatory power.

Another error of many empirical studies on the relation between religion and achievement is that they attempt to answer questions concerning historical patterns of mobility with contemporary survey data. However, factors that account for the differential rate of mobility in the past are not necessarily the ones that are most critical today. One would not test Weber's thesis concerning the reason for Protestant business success in nineteenth-century Europe by conducting a survey of Protestants in twentieth-century America. By the same token, now that immigrant groups have had several generations to establish themselves in the class system and to assimilate much of the dominant culture, it is doubtful whether contemporary patterns of ethnic stratification can be accounted for in terms of ethnic factors that operated in the distant past. Indeed, even from a historical standpoint, the value systems of ethnic groups were contingent upon social class factors, as the next chapter will show.

CULTURAL THEORIES AND THE "SIN OF REIFICATION" Ethnographic and historical studies leave no doubt that the cultures that Jewish and Catholic immigrants brought with them differed in ways that influenced their adjustment to American educational institutions. Attitudes toward education constitute the most obvious difference, and the one with most direct bearing on the question of intellectual achievement. Of course, these attitudes were embedded in a much larger cultural system, including socialization practices that assured their transmission and their integration into personality structure.

However, cultural differences between Jews and Catholics properly mark the beginning, not the end, of sociological analysis. To speak of cultural values apart from the conditions that produce and maintain them is to commit what Abraham Kaplan (1964, p. 61) calls the "sin of reification." This occurs whenever values are treated as though they have an existence all their own, independent of the material and social conditions in which they are anchored. The tendency toward reification is responsible for the illusion of a "Jewish mystique," as one sociologist recently entitled his book (Van den Haag, 1969).

Always lurking in the background of the cultural theories reviewed above was social class, broadly conceived in terms of relations to the means of production. Although Russian Jews had rich intellectual traditions, it is also true that, despite economic hardship, they were heavily concentrated in middle-class occupations. And although the attitudes of southern Italians toward formal education were distinctly antagonistic, these were the attitudes typical of peasants who are tied to the soil and living on the margin of existence.

It thus becomes necessary to further explore the relation between the cultures of Jewish and Catholic immigrants and their divergent life circumstances. The central question is this: To what extent were Jewish and Catholic attitudes toward education only epiphenomenal—that is, merely surface expressions of underlying class factors? In other words, did Jews in America disproportionately become middle class and produce a class of scholars because they placed a special value on learning? Or were they middle class first, in which case their attitudes toward education may only have been a subset within a larger system of middle-class values? The same reasoning applies to Catholics. Is their lower rate of upward mobility and academic achievement a consequence of disabling religious and cultural values? Or would it be more correct to say that Catholics started out at lower class levels and their attitudes toward education were those that generally accompany social and economic disadvantage?

4. Social Class Differences Between Jewish and Catholic Immigrants

The mystique of Jewish success, both economic and academic, stems from the assumption that Jewish and non-Jewish immigrants began life in America on an equal footing. The reasoning runs as follows: since all immigrants started out as impoverished aliens, why have the accomplishments of Jews so far surpassed all others? Thus in a recent text on minority groups in America Judith Kramer (1970, p. 115) writes, "Jewish immigrants, like most immigrants, came with few skills and no money. They started in American society as workers and peddlers, and they achieved remarkable success."

This assumption of initial parity is the basis of invidious comparisons frequently made between the impressive accomplishments of Jews and the relative failure of other groups. For example, in *American Catholic Dilemma* Thomas O'Dea (1958, p. 87) writes:

It is doubtful if even the Irish immigrants, perhaps the poorest of the nineteenth-century arrivals to these shores, were much poorer than the eastern European and Russian Jews who came after 1890, except possibly in the worst years of the Irish potato failure of the 1840s. Yet these eastern Jews . . . have contributed a larger proportion of their children and grandchildren to academic and scholarly life than have Catholic immigrants as a whole.

Having assumed that Catholics and Jews started out in the same place in the class system, O'Dea dismisses class factors as irrelevant to the question of why Jews have produced a greater number of scholars.

Other writers have suggested that although Jews started out in the lower class, they were nevertheless middle class in mentality and outlook. This view also assumes an initial parity between Jewish and non-Jewish immigrants in terms of actual class position, but asserts that Jewish *culture* was middle class, partly because of a unique religious tradition, partly because Jews were an urban people. Nathan Glazer has been the most notable exponent of this point of view:

The Jewish immigrants who came from Eastern Europe to the United States during 1881–1924 numbered as many workers and as many impoverished workers, as any other ethnic group. *But they carried with them the values conducive to middle-class success* and could, under the proper circumstances, easily return to the pursuit of trade and study, and thus to the ways of their fathers and forefathers (Glazer, 1955, pp. 31–32, italics added).[1]

All the writers quoted above correctly assume that the mass of Jewish immigrants after 1880 were impoverished. This is evident from the data in Table 1 which report the financial condition of immigrants arriving between 1904 and 1910. At the port of entry immigrants were routinely asked how much money they had in their possession; the figures refer to the proportion reporting $50 or more. As can be seen, English and Germans came with substantially greater financial resources than other groups. In contrast, only 12 percent of Jewish immigrants came with $50 or more, and although the figures for southern Italians and Poles are lower, the difference is not so great as to suggest that Jews had a decisive economic advantage. In sheer economic terms Jews resembled other immigrants, most of whom arrived nearly penniless.[2]

Despite this fact, the assumption of initial class parity between

[1] Elsewhere in the same article Glazer writes: "The Jewish immigrants still maintained a small advantage, in weekly and annual earnings, over other immigrants; but it was a very small advantage indeed. *The Jews were scarcely distinguishable from the huge mass of depressed immigrants, illiterate and impoverished, that was pouring into the United States at a rate of 1,000,000 a year before the first World War. . . .* Nevertheless, we can see that, hard pressed as they were, the Russian immigrants were, so to speak, storing up virtues for the future. Thus, we find that more of them than of other groups were learning English. Even more significant as a sign of Jewish preparation for the future was the large numbers that were going to college" (Glazer, 1955, p. 15, italics added).

[2] In at least one respect Jews probably had an economic advantage over others. Of all European immigrant groups, Jews were the most likely to report that relatives had paid for their passage. The figure for Jews was 58 percent; for southern Italians, 26 percent; for immigrants as a whole, 30 percent. This would seem to indicate that Jews received greater economic aid from earlier settlers than was the case for other immigrants (*Reports of the Immigration Commission,* 1911, p. 361).

TABLE 1
Financial
condition of
immigrants,
1904–1910

Immigrant group	Percentage reporting $50 or more upon arrival
English	55
Germans	31
Irish	17
Scandinavians	14
Northern Italians	14
Jews	12
Southern Italians	5
Poles	3
All immigrants*	14

* Includes groups not listed in the table.
SOURCE: Adapted from the *Reports of the Immigration Commission,* (vol. 3, 1911, p. 350).

Jewish and other immigrants is oversimplified and inaccurate. Most importantly, it fails to take into account noneconomic dimensions of social class. Wealth or economic position tap only one dimension. A second is measured by occupation, which even more than income defines the relationship of workers to the means of production. Education measures still another dimension of social class, and is probably more important than either income or occupation as a predictor of class mobility. No one would think of classifying an impoverished college student in the same category as an impoverished worker, if only because the student's education and occupational training assure that he will eventually improve his economic position. By the same token, if it can be shown that Jewish immigrants had marked advantages along noneconomic dimensions of social class, this would effectively invalidate widely accepted notions concerning the initial class parity between Jewish and other immigrants. It would also cast doubt on theories that explain Catholic-Jewish differences in class mobility and intellectual achievement primarily in terms of differences in cultural values and orientations.

The analysis that follows is based principally on two early studies. The first is a report entitled "The Economic Conditions of Jews in Russia" in which the author, Israel Rubinow (1907), skillfully analyzes data collected in the Russian census of 1897. The second is the 1911 *Reports of the Immigration Commission.* Established by Congress in 1907, the commission undertook an extensive series of studies of the immigration "problem." Although not always objective in its interpretations, the 41-volume report produced by the commission is nevertheless the most extensive and useful body of data that exists on the great migrations beginning in the 1880s.[3]

OCCUPATIONAL ADVANTAGES OF JEWISH IMMIGRANTS

At the turn of the twentieth century the economy of the Russian Empire was primarily agricultural. According to the 1897 census, 60 percent of the laboring force was engaged in agriculture. Partly because of legal restrictions on the ownership of land, Jews resided almost exclusively in small towns and worked in urban occupations. As Table 2 shows, 38 percent were employed in manufacturing or as artisans, and another 32 percent in commerce, making a total of 70 percent. Excluding women, the figure is 74 percent. In contrast, only 18 percent of Russia's non-Jewish population were engaged in these two fields.

Among Jews employed in manufacturing, the greatest number worked in the textile industry, most often as tailors. In the Pale —the western provinces of Russia where most Jews were required to live—this industry was almost entirely Jewish. Other Jews were engaged in the manufacture of industrial products. Despite legal restrictions, one-third of the factories in the Pale were owned by Jews, although these were mostly small enterprises. While Jews constituted only 12 percent of the total population in the Pale, they were one-fifth of all factory workers (Rubinow, 1907, pp. 497–506, 536–542).

TABLE 2
Occupations of Jews and non-Jews in Russia, 1897

Occupations	Percent		Number	
	Jews	Non-Jews	Jews	Non-Jews
Manufacturing and artisans	37.9	15.2	542,563	4,627,356
Commerce	31.6	2.7	452,193	804,137
Service	19.4	16.2	277,466	4,872,546
Professions	5.0	3.0	71,950	916,863
Transportation	3.2	2.2	45,944	688,801
Agriculture	2.9	60.5	40,611	18,204,676
TOTAL	100.0	100.0	1,430,727	30,114,379

SOURCE: Compiled from the *Premier Recensement Géneral de la Population de l'Empire de Russie, 1897.* Reported in Rubinow (1907, p. 500).

[3] For a discussion of some of the limitations and defects of the studies produced by the Immigration Commission, see Handlin (1957, Ch. 5).

Commerce in the Pale was even more heavily Jewish. Indeed, nearly three-quarters of all those employed in commerce were Jews. In some provinces, such as Lithuania and White Russia, the figure was as high as 90 percent. About half the Jews in commerce were dealers in agricultural products such as grain, cattle, hides, furs, and other commodities. They performed their legendary role as middlemen, buying farm products from the peasants and selling them again at the point of shipment or market distribution. Others were engaged as merchants or peddlers, selling to the local population.

Despite their occupational sophistication, Russian Jews were anything but prosperous. Competition was intense in the few occupations in which Jews were permitted to work, and profits were small. Rubinow (1907, p. 558) offers this description of market conditions among dealers in agricultural products:

The Jewish "merchant" whose only capital may be the price of a few bushels of corn, is more anxious to buy than the peasant is to sell, for the latter is sure of his ability to sell all he has, the question being only between a higher or lower price, while the Jew is by far not sure of his ability to buy, and it is the difference of a few cents more or less that means to him either some profit or a loss.

Nor were market conditions favorable when the dealer sold his merchandise:

Having bought the few bushels of grain or the small quantities of other agricultural products, the Jew is anxious to sell as quickly as possible, that he may recover his capital, and he sells to a merchant who is in a position to accumulate purchases of a few carloads until he is ready to ship them to the central market or to Germany (ibid., pp. 558–559).

As these passages suggest, business was typically on a very small scale with little capital accumulation. Retailers were little more than paupers: "All the available goods for sale may not be worth more than five rubles ($2.58), empty boxes, bags, and papers being artfully displayed with the intention to deceive the prospective buyer into the belief that the 'store' is really a store" (ibid., p. 561). For those who worked in factories, wages were pitifully low. Conditions varied from one region to another—for example, Jews from Lithuania were generally better off than Jews from Poland—but on the whole the condition of Russian Jews was one of extreme poverty, though not as severe as that of the peasant population.

Despite their poverty, however, Jews had experience in occupations that prepared them for roles in a modern industrial economy. This important point, often missed because of the preoccupation with the fact that Jews were poor, was well understood by the authors of a 1912 study on immigration. They wrote:

Possessed of the characteristics of a modern people in their economic and social life and in their mentality, they present a sharp contrast with the peoples among whom they dwell and whose economic and social life are only now taking on modern forms. It is this that makes the Jews personify in a large degree the forces of economic enterprise and of social progress in these countries (Jenks & Lauck, 1912, p. 54).

The fact is that Russian Jews had achieved a far higher level of occupational sophistication than most other immigrant groups prior to their arrival in America. This is clearly demonstrated in Table 3, which reports the occupations of immigrants entering the United States between 1899 and 1910. Two-thirds (67 percent) of Jewish immigrants were classified as skilled workers. The figures for each of the predominantly Catholic nationality groups is much lower: 20 percent for northern Italians; 15 percent for southern Italians; 13 percent for Irish; 6 percent for Poles.

TABLE 3
Occupations of immigrants entering the United States, 1899–1910

Previous occupation*	Jews	Northern Italians	Southern Italians	Irish	Poles
Professional	1%	1%	0%	1%	0%
Skilled worker	67	20	15	13	6
Merchant or dealer	5	1	1	1	0
Laborer	12	48	42	31	45
Farmer	2	21	35	7	31
Servant	11	8	6	46	17
Other	2	1	1	1	1
Number	590,267	296,622	1,471,659	376,268	748,430

*Excludes those without occupations, including most women and children.
SOURCE: Adapted from the *Reports of the Immigration Commission* (vol. 1, 1911, p. 100).

Jews ranked first in 26 of the 47 trades tabulated by the commission:

They constituted 80 percent of the hat and cap makers, 75 percent of the furriers, 68 percent of the tailors and bookbinders, 60 percent of the watchmakers and milliners, and 55 percent of the cigarmakers and tinsmiths. They totaled 30 to 50 percent of the immigrants classified as tanners, turners, undergarment makers, jewelers, painters, glaziers, dressmakers, photographers, saddle-makers, locksmiths, butchers, and metal workers in other than iron and steel. They ranked first among immigrant printers, bakers, carpenters, cigar-packers, blacksmiths, and building trades workmen (Rischin, 1962, p. 59).

No other immigrant group arrived with such an array of industrial skills.

Furthermore, these skills corresponded with remarkable precision to needs in the American economy. This was especially true in the apparel trades, which were undergoing a technological revolution and a period of unprecedented growth. Prior to the second half of the nineteenth century, clothing was handmade, occasionally in small shops but more frequently at home. The development of the sewing machine, however, made it feasible to mass-produce ready-made clothing for the first time. It would be difficult to exaggerate the significance of this industry for the economic adjustment of

Germans	Scandi-navians	English	All immigrants
4%	1%	9%	1%
30	20	49	20
5	0	5	2
20	36	18	36
21	11	4	25
19	30	5	14
1	2	10	2
458,293	475,094	249,998	7,048,953

Jewish immigrants. Between 1899 and 1910, 145,272 Jewish immigrants were classified as tailors; if seamstresses and other related workers are included, the figure rises to over 225,000 (*Reports of the Immigration Commission,* vol. 3, 1911, pp. 98–178). Most found employment in the expanding clothing industry, which in New York City was dominated by German Jews. As with trends in higher education, a fortuitous combination of circumstances allowed Jews to make the most of their native resources.

Russian Jews introduced an assembly-line process, called the "task system," into the clothing industry. Formerly a single tailor produced a garment from beginning to end, but with the task system the work was divided among teams consisting of one operator, one baster, one finisher, and for every three teams, two pressers. Other lesser tasks, such as buttonhole-making, were assigned to less skilled workers. Not only did this system introduce economies into the production process, but it allowed the employment of an unskilled and cheap labor force (*Reports of the Industrial Commission on Immigration,* vol. 15, 1901, pp. 317–369).

This new principle of organization also resulted in the proliferation of small shops and factories, known as the "sweating system." Essentially this was a system of contract labor whereby manufacturers farmed out work to labor contractors who employed a small number of immigrant workers in a shop or at home. In 1913 the clothing industry in New York City consisted of 16,552 such "factories," providing as many opportunities for individual entrepreneurship (Rischin, 1962, p. 66). As a report by the Industrial Commission indicated, the obstacles to entrepreneurship were not great:

These small shops are able, on account of low rent and meager wages, to compete successfully, although with foot power, against the large shops and factories with team or electric power. Usually it is not necessary to have more than $50 to start a shop with foot-power machines. As there is no investment in goods, the contractor runs no risk. Little managing ability is required because the number of employees is small (*Reports of the Industrial Commission on Immigration,* vol. 15, 1901, p. 321).

As the report went on to note, the contractor's greatest asset was his access to cheap labor supplied by his coreligionists from abroad. Thanks to the task system and the abundant supply of cheap labor, garments were produced at half their original cost. By 1914 Eastern

European Jews had replaced German Jews as the dominant element in the nation's garment industry.[4]

Similar opportunities for business entrepreneurship existed in other areas of commercial life, allowing Jewish immigrants to capitalize on their experience as peddlers, merchants, and middlemen. Despite some spectacular successes, most of these businesses remained on a small scale and simply provided an adequate living. Nevertheless, they served as a springboard for economic mobility and status enhancement in the next generation. As will presently be seen, a surprising number of Jewish scholars have their origins in this class of business entrepreneurs.

EDUCATIONAL ADVANTAGES OF JEWISH IMMIGRANTS

As stated above, social class is a composite of three factors — wealth, occupation, and education. It has already been established that although Jews had no initial advantage over other immigrants in terms of wealth, they did possess superior occupational skills that facilitated their economic adjustment. In addition, Jewish immigrants had educational advantages over most other immigrant groups. As with occupation, a contemporary yardstick would not be sensitive to the kinds of differences that existed. Jews in Russia were generally excluded from state schools and usually received their education in religious schools. Many others were educated outside any institutional context. Thus in terms of formal education, differences between Jews and other immigrants may not be great. However, when literacy is used as a standard of comparison, substantial differences appear.

Even in Russia the rate of literacy for Jews was almost twice the national average. According to the 1897 census, the rate of literacy for those 10 years or older was 50 percent for Jews as compared to 28 percent for non-Jews. In both cases males had a higher rate of literacy than females. Among males the figure is 65 percent for Jews, 39 percent for non-Jews. Even more striking is the fact that literacy was higher among Jewish males over 60 years of age than for non-Jewish males between 10 and 19. The rates were 54 percent

---

[4] "By 1914 the industry's personnel had changed. Except in the older and more heavily capitalized men's clothing industry, employers were no longer of German Jewish stock, as they had been before the turn of the century, but now were overwhelmingly East Europeans. Employees too, once predominantly English, Irish, and German, except for the men's clothing cutters, were now East European Jews" (Rischin, 1962, p. 67). For a valuable fictional account, see Cahan (1960).

and 46 percent, respectively. As Rubinow (1907, p. 578) remarked: ". . . fifty years ago the educational standard of the Jews was higher than that of the Russian people . . . at present."

The figures reported above refer to an ability to read Yiddish, the native tongue of Russian Jews. However, even in Russian the rate of literacy was higher among Jews than among non-Jews. The 1897 census reported 32 percent of Jews could read Russian, as compared to 28 percent of non-Jews. Excluding women, the figures are 43 percent and 39 percent.

Table 4 now compares rates of illiteracy among European immigrants entering the country between 1899 and 1910. Illiteracy was the exception among immigrants from Western Europe, never exceeding 5 percent for any nationality. The rate is also low for immigrants from northern Italy (12 percent), but most Italian immigrants came from the South and among this group the rate of illiteracy was 54 percent. In contrast, the Jewish rate was only half as great — 26 percent.

TABLE 4		
Rates of illiteracy of European immigrants, 1899–1910 (immigrants over 14 years of age)		

Immigrant groups	Percentage illiterate*	Number
Jews	26	806,786
Northern Italians	12	339,301
Southern Italians	54	1,690,376
Irish	3	416,640
Poles	35	861,303
Germans	5	625,793
Scandinavians	1	530,634
English	1	347,458
All immigrants	27	8,398,624

*Refers to an inability to read or write.

SOURCE: Adapted from the *Reports of the Immigration Commission*, vol. 1, 1911, p. 99).

For an immigrant in an alien country, literacy was an obvious asset and the low rate of literacy among southern Italians was one factor retarding their cultural assimilation. Another factor was that most Italians initially immigrated as sojourners rather than as permanent settlers. Typically they left their families behind, and once they accumulated some savings they voyaged back across the

Atlantic.[5] In contrast, having been driven out of Russia by religious persecution and political violence, few Jews entertained thoughts of returning. This helps to make sense of the fact that Italian immigrants were much slower to become naturalized or even to learn English.[6]

Table 5 shows the rate at which different immigrant groups learned to speak English. Among Russian Jews with less than five years residence in the United States, 65 percent spoke English. The figures for northern and southern Italians are only half as great—34 and 27 percent. With longer residence Italians gradually closed the gap, but even after a period of 10 years southern Italians were less likely to speak English than any other immigrant group.

TABLE 5
Ability of foreign-born industrial workers to speak English by years in the United States*

Foreign-born industrial workers	Number of years in the United States			
	Less than 5	*5–9*	*10 or more*	*Total*
	Percentage that speak English			
Russian Jews	65	81	88	75
Other Jews	67	85	89	81
Northern Italians	34	70	85	56
Southern Italians	27	59	73	44
Polish	18	46	75	39
German	49	81	95	84
Swedish	73	95	99	95
All immigrants (from non-English-speaking countries)	29	60	83	53

* The data are based on large surveys of wage earners in 37 principal branches of mining and manufacturing in the United States.
SOURCE: Adapted from the *Reports of the Immigration Commission* vol. 23, 1911, p. 197).

[5] That Italians more often came as temporary workers is indicated by the fact that there were relatively few females and children among them. Between 1899 and 1910, only 21 percent of southern Italian immigrants were female, as compared to 43 percent among Jews. The proportion of children under 14 years of age was 12 percent for southern Italians, 25 percent for Jews. The clearest indication that Italians were often sojourners rather than permanent settlers is indicated by figures on the rate returning to the country of origin. For every 100 southern Italians admitted between 1908 and 1910, there were 55 departures; the comparable figure for Jews is only 8 (*Reports of the Immigration Commission,* vol. 1, 1911, pp. 97, 113).

[6] "The essential characteristic of the sojourner is that he clings to his own ethnic group as in contrast to the bicultural complex of the marginal man" (Siu, 1952, p. 36).

The reluctance of Italians to learn English was often noted with indignation by contemporaries. In 1890 Jacob Riis wrote unsympathetically of the Italian: "He not only knows no word of English, but he does not know enough to learn. Rarely only can he write his own language. Unlike the German, who begins learning English the day he lands as a matter of duty, or the Polish Jew, who takes it up as soon as he is able as an investment, the Italian learns slowly, if at all" (Riis, 1957, p. 87). Despite Riis' obvious bias, it is true that the pace of cultural accommodation was slower for Italians than for most other immigrant groups. This in turn had ramifications for the education of Italian children—whether they stayed in school and how well they performed academically—as the next section now demonstrates.

THE CHILDREN OF IMMIGRANTS IN THE SCHOOLS

In 1908 the U.S. Immigration Commission conducted a massive survey of schoolchildren in cities with large immigrant populations ("The Children of Immigrants in Schools," 1911). The enumeration included over 2 million schoolchildren, although most of the results reported below are based on a more intensive investigation of 61,000 pupils in 12 cities. Ostensibly the survey was undertaken "to determine . . . to what extent immigrant children are availing themselves of educational facilities and what progress they make in school work" (ibid., p. 3). Other less exalted motives were probably involved, judging from the final report which seemed bent on showing that children of the "new immigration" did not perform well in schools. Nevertheless, the vast body of data collected by the commission reveals a great deal about why Jewish children achieved a far better academic record than children from other nationality backgrounds.

The focus of the commission's report was on the extent and causes of "retardation." It is important to note that this term in no way refers to a mental disorder. In the study retardation was defined as being two or more years older than the average age for a particular grade. Today such students would be called "underachievers" or "slow learners." Of course, in some cases retardation may only have reflected the fact that students were forced to work periodically and fell behind their grade level on this account. Indeed, this practice was particularly common among lower-class Italians who often needed and expected their children to contribute to the family income.

As Table 6 shows, the rate of retardation for native whites was

28 percent. This figure establishes a minimal level of retardation irrespective of immigration and is therefore a benchmark against which other groups can be compared. Interestingly enough, the rate of retardation for children of immigrants from English-speaking countries was no higher than that for the native-born. In contrast, the rate for children of immigrants from non-English-speaking countries was 43 percent.

TABLE 6
Rates of retardation for children of immigrants (children 8 years of age or over)

Immigrant groups	Percentage retarded*	Number
German Jews	37	231
Russian Jews	42	5,484
Romanian Jews	52	241
Polish Jews	67	154
Northern Italians	52	550
Southern Italians	64	2,978
Irish	29	932
Polish	58	1,212
German	33	4,137
Swedish	16	1,247
English	26	2,086
Native-born whites	28	16,881
English-speaking foreign-born	27	5,295
Non-English-speaking foreign-born	43	10,252

* A retarded pupil is defined as one who is two or more years older than the average age for his grade.
SOURCE: Adapted from "The Children of Immigrants in Schools," (vol. 1, 1911, p. 31).

Italian and Irish Catholics are at opposite extremes. Italians have one of the highest rates of retardation—52 percent in the case of northern Italians, 64 percent in the case of southern Italians. On the other hand, children of Irish immigrants exhibit the lowest rate of any immigrant group—29 percent. Ethnic variation is just as great among Jews as among Catholics. The rate of retardation ranges from 37 percent among German Jews, 42 percent among Russian Jews, 52 percent among Romanian Jews, to 67 percent among Polish Jews. Indeed, the rate for Romanian Jews is equal to that for northern Italians, and the rate for Polish Jews is roughly the same as that for southern Italians.

If rates of retardation had been examined by religion, Catholic children would have appeared far more likely than Jewish children to be behind their grade level in school. However, Table 6 implies that this difference is a function of the ethnic composition of each group. In 1908, when the survey was conducted, most foreign-born Jews were Russian, whereas most foreign-born Catholics were Italian. It appears that this ethnic factor is more important than religion as a determinant of academic achievement among their children.

Without further evidence, it is impossible to know whether these findings can be generalized to higher levels of the academic ladder. However, it is apparent that most Jewish scholars have come from German and Russian, rather than Romanian and Polish, backgrounds. There is also good reason to think that Irish and German Catholics have produced more scholars than have Italians or Poles.[7] If this is true, then important theoretical implications follow. It means that Catholic-Jewish differences in intellectual achievement may be less a product of differences in religious traditions and values than in the ethnic composition of each group. Although this would not necessarily render religion as insignificant, it does shift the focus of attention away from purely religious factors and toward the conditions and historical experiences of Jewish and Catholic immigrants in their countries of origin.

Earlier it was suggested that the acculturation process was faster and less problematic for Jews than for other immigrant groups, especially Italians. Jews started out as a more literate group, they emigrated with the aim of settling permanently in America, and less time passed before they learned English and became naturalized. The commission's studies show that these factors had direct consequences for the school performance of immigrant children. As Table 7 shows, in every immigrant group children were more likely to fall behind in school if their parents did not have naturalization papers, if they did not speak English, and if they did not speak English at home. Moreover, among children with these handicaps in their family background, rates of retardation were almost as high among Russian Jews as among southern Italians. For example, among

[7] This can be inferred from the relative levels of educational attainment of Catholic ethnic groups. On the basis of a 1963 national survey of Catholics, Greeley (1971, p. 67) reports that the proportion of Catholics who had completed high school varied as follows: Irish, 77 percent; Germans, 62 percent; Italians, 51 percent; Poles, 46 percent; French, 42 percent.

children whose fathers did not speak English, the rate of retardation was 67 percent for Jews and 73 percent for southern Italians. On the other hand, among those whose fathers did speak English, there is a very large difference between the two groups. Among southern Italians retardation is still high—59 percent; but among Russian Jews it drops to 35 percent, almost as low as among native Americans (28 percent).

TABLE 7
Retardation by extent of parents' acculturation

Immigrant group	Fathers have naturalization papers?		Fathers speak English?		English spoken at home?	
	Yes	*No*	*Yes*	*No*	*Yes*	*No*
	Percentage retarded					
Germans	32	43	32	41	30	37
Russian Jews	36	59	35	67	33	51
Southern Italians	60	71	59	73	56	67

SOURCE: Adapted from "The Children of Immigrants in Schools" (vol. 1, 1911, pp. 35–36).

These data have indicated three things: 1) as compared to Italians, Russian Jews show signs of more rapid acculturation; 2) for Jews and Italians alike, lack of acculturation led to retardation in a majority of cases; and 3) unlike Jews, even when Italian children came from families that were acculturated, they tended to fall behind in school.

In a sense the commission's measure of retardation is itself an indicator of acculturation. Parity between the children of an immigrant group and native children in the public schools indicates at least one significant way in which that immigrant group had completed the process of adjustment. Thus by examining the relationship between retardation and the amount of time immigrants have been in the United States, as is done in Table 8, we are in effect observing the differential rates of acculturation of different ethnic groups.

At one extreme are immigrants from England. For them acculturation was not problematic, and even among recent immigrants the rate of retardation is relatively low—31 percent as compared to 28 percent among native children. Sharing the same language and cultural tradition, assimilation is immediate and complete. German and Russian Jews constitute a second type. Among the children of recent immigrants (those with less than five years in this

Length of residence	English	Germans	Russian Jews	Southern Italians
		Percentage retarded		
Under 5 years	31	67	75	82
5–9 years	26	42	57	75
10–19 years	23	33	32	62
20 years or more	26	31	30	55

SOURCE: Adapted from "The Children of Immigrants in Schools," (vol. 1, 1911, p. 36).

country), the rates of retardation are very high—67 percent for Germans and 75 percent for Russians. However, among older settlers the rates drop off sharply. Children whose fathers had been in the country from 10 to 19 years exhibit a rate of retardation only slightly higher than that of native Americans. As compared to Russian Jews, German Jews started off with a somewhat lower rate of retardation and it drops off somewhat faster, but both groups end up with the same low rate of retardation after 10 years of residence.

Southern Italians represent a third type. Among recent immigrants the level of retardation is not much higher than that of Russian Jews. However, the rate declines much more slowly over time. Thus even among Italian children whose fathers had settled 20 or more years earlier, the rate of retardation is 55 percent. In short, it took southern Italians more than 20 years to reduce retardation to the level that Russian Jews achieved in only five to nine years.

One qualification, however: Even among southern Italians the rates of retardation decline steadily with longer settlement, and as Table 8 shows, the difference between Italians and Jews begins to diminish after 20 years. If one assumes that this trend continued after 1908, the year the data were collected, then this would create a pattern of ever-diminishing differences between Italians and Jews (as must happen since the figures for Jews bottomed out earlier while those for Italians continued a gradual decline). As will be seen in the next chapter, much the same pattern has occurred with respect to Jewish and Catholic representation in higher education: as the Jewish proportion reaches its peak, Catholics gradually are closing the gap.

A 1922 study of high school students in Bridgeport, Connecticut, produced findings consistent with those of the Immigration Commission (Counts, 1922, p. 108). In this case the measure of academic achievement was the number of students in the senior year for every 100 in the freshman year; this provides a crude estimate of the drop-out rates for different ethnic groups. In the case of native Americans there were 44 seniors for every 100 freshmen. For children of Russian immigrants, most of whom were Jews, there were 51 seniors for every 100 freshmen. Interestingly enough, the figure for Irish was almost as great—48. In contrast, among children of Italian immigrants there were only 17 seniors for every 100 freshmen. In the case of Poles the figure was 15. As in the 1908 studies, Irish closely resembled Jews in school performance whereas Italians fell far behind both groups (ibid.). This is perhaps the strongest indication that ethnic factors weighed more heavily than religious ones in producing an underrepresentation of Catholics on higher levels of the academic ladder.

CLASS ORIGINS OF CONTEMPORARY AMERICAN SCHOLARS The image of children from working-class Jewish backgrounds "making it" to the heights of academe pervades both popular legend and social science. However, its validity is thrown into question by many of the historical findings reported above. It has been established that although the economic position of Jewish immigrants was initially comparable to that of other groups, Jews possessed the prerequisites of mobility in the form of occupational skills and literacy. It was further demonstrated that the high rate of literacy and the rapid pace of cultural accommodation among Jewish immigrants helped to explain the relative success of their children in the schools. By extension this implies that the social class advantages of Jewish immigrants also may be the reason for the historic representation of Jews, and the underrepresentation of Catholics, among the nation's scholars and scientists.

This theory can be put to a simple empirical test. If it turns out that earlier generations of Jewish faculty came disproportionately from the working class, then this would invalidate the idea that social class advantage was of much significance in explaining Jewish academic success. On the other hand, if earlier generations of Jewish faculty came disproportionately from middle-class backgrounds, then this would suggest that social class factors were indeed crucial.

The data for the analysis that follows are derived from the Carnegie Commission Studies of Higher Education. The sample consists of approximately 60,000 faculty in 303 institutions of higher learning who responded to a mail questionnaire in the spring of 1969. The size of the sample fortunately allows analysis of special subgroups such as older Jewish and Catholic faculty, who provide clear evidence of the social class background of the postimmigration generation of scholars.[8]

Table 9 reports the occupation of the fathers of Protestant, Catholic, and Jewish faculty, controlling for age. The category labeled "working class" includes workers in white-collar occupations with

TABLE 9
*Class origins of
all faculty by
religion and age*

Religious background	Age				
	55+	*45–54*	*35–44*	*34—*	*Total*
Protestants					
Professional	26%	22%	22%	25%	23%
*Managerial**	13	16	17	20	17
Owner—small business	17	16	15	13	15
Farm	19	14	12	9	13
Working class†	25	32	34	33	32
Number‡	46,199	65,740	85,411	87,541	285,502
Catholics					
Professional	10%	14%	13%	16%	14%
Managerial	19	18	19	22	20
Owner—small business	22	16	17	13	16
Farm	9	6	5	4	5
Working class	40	46	46	45	45
Number	9,052	16,023	26,048	28,644	80,010
Jews					
Professional	13%	14%	17%	26%	19%
Managerial	14	11	13	17	14
Owner—small business	52	45	44	33	41
Farm	2	1	0	1	1
Working class	19	29	26	23	25
Number	3,306	7,845	12,807	13,393	37,438

* Includes owners of large businesses.

† Includes skilled and unskilled workers and low-level white-collar workers such as clerical and sales workers. Armed Forces personnel are also included, though they constitute a negligible 1 percent of the sample.

‡ Weighted projections to the total population of faculty in American colleges and universities.

[8] Other details about the sample can be found in the introduction to Part 3 of this study.

low prestige, such as clerical and sales workers, as well as those in blue-collar occupations. In the sample as a whole the proportion of faculty with origins in the working class is lowest for Jews (25 percent), intermediate for Protestants (32 percent), and highest for Catholics (45 percent). This ranking is not surprising since it reflects the relative positions of the three religious groups in the general society.

What is surprising is that even among older age cohorts relatively few Jewish faculty come from working-class backgrounds — among those 55 or over, only 19 percent do so, in comparison to 25 percent of Protestants and 39 percent of Catholics. The next age group — those between 45 and 54 — is perhaps the most important. Born between 1914 and 1923, this group presumably has the greatest number of first- and second-generation Jews, given the upsurge of Jewish immigration that began in 1881 and reached its peak in 1913. Indeed, of all age groups this one has the highest proportion of Jewish faculty from working-class backgrounds — 29 percent. However, this figure is slightly lower than that for Protestants in the same age cohort (32 percent), and substantially lower than that for Catholics (46 percent). It is evident that, in comparison to Catholics, Jewish faculty have never come from the lowest strata of the class system.

This pattern has been modified among succeeding age cohorts. Fewer of the younger Jewish faculty have fathers who own small businesses, and more come from professional backgrounds. In part this trend reflects a general decline of small businesses in the society and can be observed to a lesser extent among Protestant and Catholic faculty as well. Nevertheless, even among the youngest Jewish faculty a third have fathers who were small entrepreneurs. As observed earlier, many Jewish immigrants were able to exploit their prior experience in commerce as an avenue of mobility. As the data now indicate, this class of business entrepreneurs also has been a principal source of scholars and scientists. On the other hand, the Jewish working class has never been a major source of Jewish scholars.

The pattern is quite the opposite for Catholics. In every age cohort roughly 4 out of every 10 Catholics come from working-class backgrounds. If anything, the legendary image of the scholar rising out of the working class fits Catholics far more often than it does Jews.

One might suppose that a different picture would emerge if only scholars of distinction were examined. Perhaps Jews in this select group disproportionately have origins in the working class. To test this possibility Table 10 examines the same combination of variables as in Table 9, but does so only for faculty in the 17 ranking universities.[9]

Like the student bodies, the faculty of the prestigious univer-

TABLE 10
Class origins of faculty in the 17 ranking universities by religion and age

Religious background	Age				
	55+	*45–54*	*35–44*	*34—*	*Total*
Protestants					
Professional	35%	33%	32%	31%	32%
Managerial	16	20	24	25	22
Owner—small business	17	16	14	14	15
Farm	12	9	6	6	8
Working class	20	22	24	24	23
Number	5,542	6,975	9,189	8,959	30,712
Catholics					
Professional	31%	22%	22%	24%	24%
Managerial	13	18	22	29	22
Owner—small business	19	14	18	13	15
Farm	6	6	4	2	4
Working class	31	40	34	34	35
Number	701	1,156	2,148	2,576	6,635
Jews					
Professional	18%	18%	20%	29%	23%
Managerial	17	11	14	16	14
Owner—small business	51	50	43	38	43
Farm	0	0	0	0	0
Working class	14	21	23	17	20
Number	801	1,704	3,143	3,006	8,761

[9] The quality rating is based upon *The Gourman Report* (Gourman, 1967). The 17 ranking universities are as follows: Brandeis University, Columbia University, Harvard University, Johns Hopkins University, Northwestern University, Princeton University, Stanford University, Tulane University, University of California at Berkeley, University of California at Los Angeles, University of Illinois, University of Michigan, University of North Carolina, University of Pennsylvania, University of Rochester, University of Washington, and Vanderbilt University.

sities tend to be drawn from the more established and affluent seg-
ments of society. This can be easily seen by juxtaposing Table 10
on Table 9. Except for this difference, however, the same patterns
emerge in the ranking universities as in higher education as a whole.
In every age group, Catholics have the highest proportion of faculty
with working-class origins. Protestant faculty have always come
disproportionately from the professional and business classes.
In the case of Jews, the route of mobility has typically begun in the
class of small businessmen, though in recent years Jewish faculty
increasingly have come from professional backgrounds. The major
conclusion, however, is that it is Catholic and not Jewish scholars
who more often have made the legendary transition from rags to
academic gown.

CONCLUSION The first three chapters of this book made it clear that Catholic
and Jewish immigrants started life in America with radically different value orientations with respect to education and intellectual
achievement. One has only to contrast the enthusiasm with which
Jews pursued education with the doubts and uncertainties that
plagued Catholics to conclude that these value differences existed
and help to explain differences between the two groups in economic
mobility and intellectual achievement.

What is at issue here is not whether Jews and Catholics differed
in their cultural values, but rather the relationship between these
cultural values and social structure. The main point of this chapter
is that Jewish and Catholic values were more than aspects of a culture passed on from one generation to the next. Their cultural
values did not exist in a vacuum. Nor were they embalmed in
cultural and historical tradition. Rather they were solidly grounded
in material conditions, particularly those associated with social
class.

Jewish immigrants were not simply middle class in their values,
as other writers have suggested. There was substance and reality
behind these values. Jews did not simply have aspirations for
economic mobility—they also had experiences and skills in middle-
class occupations. Nor did Jews simply value education and revere
learning. They were also literate as a group and had cognitive skills
to pass on to their children. Conversely, Catholics did not simply
place low value on education and occupational mobility, but were
handicapped by factors related to their peasant origins.

In short, the value orientations of both Catholics and Jews were congruent with and bolstered by social class factors. If this reasoning is correct, then changes in these underlying conditions ought to produce corresponding changes in the surface culture. Catholics provide a good test of this proposition. In this century the bulk of Irish and Italian immigrants have improved their relative class standing and, despite qualifications, are fairly well integrated into the nation's economic and cultural mainstream (Glenn & Hyland, 1967). To what extent has this resulted in changes with respect to academic achievement? Are Catholics entering the physical and social sciences to a greater extent than in the past? Do religious values continue to function as an obstacle to scholarly productivity? These questions preoccupy Part 3 of this study.

Part Three

Religious Trends in Contemporary Higher Education

Part III shifts from a historical to a contemporary perspective. Instead of historical data, it employs data from recent surveys of American higher education. These surveys complement the historical analysis of previous chapters in at least two ways. In the first place, they constitute a remarkably detailed record of contemporary higher education and, in effect, update and complete the historical trend. In the second place, the age breakdowns among faculty are themselves indicative of broad historical trends.

Thus, Chapters 5 and 6 examine trends with respect to the religious composition of academic institutions and academic disciplines. Are Jews as well represented among younger faculty as among earlier generations? Is there a trend toward greater Catholic representation? Is there a greater religious mix in academic disciplines, or are traditional patterns of religious concentration holding up?

Chapter 7 raises a different set of questions concerning the individual's religious commitments and their consequences. What are the religious commitments of American academics? Are faculty with strong religious commitments less productive as scholars? Are there signs of a special incompatibility between religion and scholarship among Catholics?

Chapter 8 then examines the larger matrix of values and attitudes of which religion forms one part. What role does religion play in the different political tendencies of Protestant, Catholic, and Jewish scholars? Is religion significant for scholarship once separated from this larger cluster of attitudes? To what extent do differences in religious involvement entail differences in perspective regarding the purposes and functions of higher education?

The data employed throughout Part III are derived from major surveys of faculty and students in the nation's universities and colleges. These surveys, sponsored by the Carnegie Commission on Higher Education, were conducted in the spring and fall of 1969. For the purposes of the present study the faculty survey was of greatest utility. Data on graduate students and undergraduates are used sparingly, usually with the purpose of assessing future trends among faculty.

The faculty sample is a disproportionate random sample consisting of 60,028 members of the teaching faculty in 303 institutions of higher learning. Weights were applied in order to adjust for the overrepresentation of high-quality universities in the original sample and unequal rates of response.[1] The overall response rate was 60 percent, typical of surveys employing mail questionnaires. An extensive analysis of nonrespondents did not reveal any significant differences between respondents and nonrespondents. Thus there is every reason for confidence that the weighted data accurately represent the total population of faculty in the nation's colleges and universities.[2]

[1] The raw figures reported in the tables are weighted projections to the total population. The actual number of cases on which percentages are based is not reported since the size of the sample assures that the number will be adequate to yield stable percentages.

[2] Further details on these surveys are found in Trow, et al. (1971); and Feldman (1974).

5. The Changing Religious Composition of American Higher Education

Even the most casual observer has some notion about the intellectual prominence of Jews in higher education. However, like most such ideas, this one is subject to ambiguity and distortion. What does "Jewish prominence" in higher education consist of? Since Jews constitute only 3 percent of the national population, they could hardly form more than a small part of faculty and students in the nation's 2,300 institutions of higher learning. "Jewish prominence" could refer to the high representation of Jews in the better institutions. But, once again, the small size of the Jewish population makes it improbable that Jews would constitute more than a small minority. It could refer to a concentration of Jews in just a few leading institutions or in a few disciplines, in which case the meaning of "prominence" is seriously qualified. Finally, it could refer only to the fact that a disproportionate number of leading scholars and scientists have been Jewish, which would circumscribe the meaning of the term even more (Levitan, 1960; Weyl & Possony, 1963, pp. 123–128). Exactly what is meant by "Jewish prominence" is itself far from clear: different people mean different things and the various meanings are often confused.

The confusion with respect to "Catholic underachievement" takes a somewhat different form. Past surveys have shown Catholics to be poorly represented among scholars and scientists of distinction (Huntington & Whitney, 1927; Lehman & Witty, 1931). Other studies have documented the poor academic record of Catholic colleges (Knapp & Goodrich, 1952; Knapp & Greenbaum, 1953). Confusion sets in when these findings are used as a basis for generalizing about Catholic "anti-intellectualism." Catholics could be broadly represented in the academic community even if they are underrepresented among scholars of distinction. And it is obviously invalid to make inferences about the academic record of Catholics in secular institutions on the basis of observations about Catholic colleges. Consequently, a matter of first importance for this study is to establish exactly what the facts are concerning the representation and distribution of Catholics and Jews in higher education.

THE RELIGIOUS DISTRIBUTION IN HIGHER EDUCATION: AN OVERVIEW

According to the best available estimates, the religious distribution of the United States is as follows:[1]

Protestants	66%
Catholics	26
Jews	3
Other religions	1
No religion	3
Not reported	1

This constitutes one standard for assessing the religious distribution in higher education. Of course, the mere fact that a religious group is overrepresented or underrepresented in terms of its national proportion cannot be assumed to be the result of religion as such. For example, Jews are disproportionately urban and middle class, and these factors would produce higher rates of college attendance even if no distinctively religious factors were at work. Nevertheless, it makes good descriptive sense to know how many Protestants, Catholics, and Jews there are at various levels of higher education, and to examine these figures against the overall religious distribution in the national population.

Table 11 shows the religious breakdown of faculty, graduate students, and undergraduates. Caution should be used not to make inferences about religious trends from these figures. The fact that the proportion of Catholics decreases as one goes up the academic ladder could mean one of two things. It could mean that Catholics

[1] U.S. Bureau of the Census (1958). There is little or no distortion resulting from the fact that 1957 figures are used as a standard of comparison. The birthrate of Catholics is presently only slightly higher than the national average, and could not significantly alter the overall religious composition of the nation in only a 20-year period. This is also indicated by surveys conducted since 1957. For example, a 1964 national survey found that Catholics were 25.8 percent of the national population, as compared to 25.7 percent reported in the 1957 census (Selznick & Steinberg, 1969).

are increasingly going to college; if this were true, then we might anticipate a rise in the proportion of Catholic faculty as undergraduates and graduates advance through the system. Or it could mean that Catholic undergraduates are less likely to go on to graduate school and Catholic graduates are less likely to become faculty, in which case no such increase in Catholic representation would be in the offing. This issue will be ironed out once the basic distribution is examined.

Table 11 reports two sets of figures. Those in the top half simply refer to the percentage distribution, while those in the bottom half show the "Index of Representation" for each group. This is the ratio between the proportion in the national population and the proportion at a particular level of higher education. Thus a ratio of 100 indicates an exact correspondence between these two figures. Ratios above 100 indicate the extent of overrepresentation; ratios under 100 the extent of underrepresentation.

TABLE 11
The religious distribution in the nation and in higher education

Religious background	Nation	Faculty	Graduates	Under-graduates
Protestant	66.2%	66.0%	57.6%	58.4%
Catholic	25.7	18.5	25.1	29.3
Jewish	3.2	8.7	10.0	5.3
Other	1.3	3.6	3.6	4.2
None	2.7	3.2	3.7	2.8
Number	119,333,000	434,104	974,987	907,131
*Index of representation**				
Protestant	100	100	87	88
Catholic	100	72	98	114
Jewish	100	272	312	166

*The ratio of the proportion in higher education against the proportion in the national population.

This measure shows that Catholics are underrepresented among faculty. However, among graduate students Catholics are represented in exactly their proportion in the national population, and among undergraduates they are actually overrepresented. The percentage figures are 18, 25, and 29 percent, respectively.

In contrast, Jews are substantially overrepresented among all three groups. Their overrepresentation is greatest among graduate students, partly reflecting the high proportion of Jews in professional schools. If Jewish representation is lowest among undergraduates, it is not because fewer Jews attend college, but rather because their numbers are swamped by the sheer size of undergraduate education. Among faculty, Jews constitute 9 percent of the total, a figure that is small in absolute terms but large in relation to the number of Jews in the national population.

Finally, the proportion of Protestants among faculty is the same as in the nation as a whole—66 percent—but Protestants are somewhat underrepresented among graduate students and undergraduates. As will presently be seen, this reflects a long-term historical trend of diminishing Protestant representation at all levels of American higher education.

INSTITU- TIONAL QUALITY The figures just examined give the impression that while Jews are overrepresented in higher education, they still make up only a small portion of the total pool of faculty and students. Catholics, on the other hand, do not appear so much underrepresented as past discussions on "Catholic anti-intellectualism" would suggest. However, both these impressions are modified once institutional quality is brought into the picture. Table 12 distinguishes between universities and colleges of high, medium, and low rank, and junior colleges.[2] Of particular interest are the 17 highest-ranking universities represented in the column on the extreme left. The religious composition of faculty in these institutions is 60 percent Protestant, 13 percent Catholic, and 17 percent Jewish. Thus in comparison to their overall representation in higher education (column on the extreme right), Protestants are slightly underrepresented in ranking universities, Catholics are substantially underrepresented, and Jews are substantially overrepresented. Persons who reported their religious background as "none" also are overrepresented, but are small in number.

It is noteworthy that the extent of Catholic underrepresentation in the ranking universities is not as great among students as among faculty. This can be observed by computing the ratio between the proportion of Catholics in ranking universities and the proportion in the total population of faculty or students. Among faculty this ratio is only 71; among graduate students it increases to 80; among

[2]The basic source of the quality rating is *The Gourman Report* (Gourman, 1967). For a list of the 17 ranking universities, see footnote 9 in Ch. 4.

TABLE 12 *The religious distribution in higher education by institutional quality*

	Universities			Colleges			Junior colleges	Total
	High	Medium	Low	High	Medium	Low		
Faculty								
Protestants	59.9%	63.1%	69.3%	64.7%	66.7%	67.1%	69.9%	66.0%
Catholics	13.2	14.7	16.7	13.4	22.7	23.8	20.5	18.5
Jews	17.2	14.8	7.2	13.2	6.3	3.3	3.4	8.7
Other	3.9	3.4	3.9	4.2	2.2	3.7	3.8	3.6
None	5.8	4.0	2.9	4.5	2.1	2.1	2.4	3.2
Number	54,399	78,796	68,522	24,648	47,646	97,055	63,042	434,104
Graduate students								
Protestants	53.7%	54.3%	61.0%	48.4%	62.8%	61.3 %		57.6%
Catholics	20.0	24.3	24.8	22.2	29.1	29.8		25.1
Jews	16.0	14.6	6.5	13.1	3.9	4.9		10.1
Other	4.4	3.3	4.6	10.5	1.6	1.3		3.5
None	5.9	3.5	3.1	5.8	2.6	2.7		3.7
Number	167,089	24,992	216,139	58,156	115,994	167,615		974,987
Undergraduates								
Protestants	43.2%	57.6%	57.0%	65.2%	62.8%	57.2%	59.7%	58.4%
Catholics	26.7	26.0	29.8	17.6	29.6	33.7	28.2	29.3
Jews	20.1	10.9	7.9	10.1	4.0	3.7	2.6	5.3
Other	4.5	4.0	3.9	4.1	1.8	4.2	4.9	4.2
None	5.5	1.5	1.4	3.0	1.8	1.2	4.6	2.8
Number	34,369	80,224	113,068	26,810	86,253	223,359	341,176	907,131

undergraduates it increases again to 91. Thus not only does Catholic representation increase at lower academic levels, but the extent of underrepresentation in the better institutions also grows smaller.

The extent of Jewish concentration in the 17 ranking universities is indeed striking: Jews constitute 17 percent of faculty, 16 percent of graduate students, and 20 percent of undergraduates. On the other hand, in the lowest-ranking colleges the proportion of Jews hardly exceeds their proportion in the population: Jews are 3 percent of faculty, 5 percent of graduate students, and 4 percent of undergraduates.

Also noteworthy is the high proportion of Protestants in the undergraduate bodies of high-ranking colleges (65 percent as compared to just 43 percent in high-ranking universities). These are primarily the Eastern elite colleges, many of which were funded by Protestant denominations and have managed to maintain a solid Protestant majority in their undergraduate bodies.

Table 12 raises two questions that warrant further analysis. The first concerns the reasons for the Jewish overrepresentation, especially in the ranking universities. Does this indicate superior performance on the part of Jews, or does it reflect economic advantage or some other factor? The second question concerns the finding that the Catholic representation is greatest among undergraduates and smallest among faculty. Does this indicate a trend for Catholics to enter higher education in greater numbers, or does it reflect a tendency for Catholic students to avoid academic careers and to enter other occupations instead? Let us address the second of these questions first.

RELIGIOUS TRENDS IN HIGHER EDUCATION

As already mentioned, the fact that the proportion of Catholics increases as one goes down the academic ladder could signify either success or failure: it could indicate a trend toward increased Catholic representation or it could mean that Catholics disproportionately terminate their academic careers at lower levels. This issue can easily be resolved by inspecting the religious distribution among faculty of different ages, as is done in Table 13.

These data show a definite upward trend in Catholic representation among faculty. Catholics make up 15 percent of the oldest age cohort, and this figure increases with younger age to 17, 19, and 20 percent. Among graduate students who say they plan a career in college teaching, the figure again rises to 22 percent.

TABLE 13
Religious background by age among faculty in all institutions

Religious background	Age of faculty				Graduate students planning a career in college teaching
	55+	45–54	35–44	34—	
Protestant	75.7%	69.0%	63.2%	62.6%	57.8%
Catholic	14.8	16.9	19.2	20.5	22.2
Jewish	5.5	8.2	9.5	9.6	9.6
Other	2.1	2.9	4.4	3.9	4.5
None	1.9	3.0	3.7	3.4	5.9
Number	61,258	95,639	135,666	140,391	257,000
Index of representation					
Protestant	144	104	96	95	87
Catholic	57	66	75	80	86
Jewish	172	256	297	300	300

As the bottom half of Table 13 shows, the Index of Representation among the oldest age cohort is just 57, indicating that Catholics were represented only about half as often as one would expect on the basis of their numbers in the national population. With younger age, however, this ratio increases—from 57 to 66 to 75 to 80. Among graduate students with academic plans the ratio again increases to 86. In short, Catholics are rapidly approaching the point of being represented among faculty in the same proportion as in the nation as a whole.[3]

If Catholic underrepresentation is rapidly becoming a thing of the past, it is because the aspirations and career plans of Catholic students are not substantially different from those of students generally. The proportion of graduate students who say they plan a career in college teaching is 35 percent for Protestants, 31 percent for Catholics, and 33 percent for Jews.[4] In the ranking universities the proportions are uniformly higher, but there is even less difference by religion: 42 percent of Protestants have academic intentions, as compared to 44 percent of Catholics and 43 percent of Jews. In other words, not only are Catholics entering graduate schools in increasing numbers, but they are just as likely to plan careers as scholars.

In the undergraduate survey students were asked what was the highest degree they hoped to attain. The proportion aspiring to a Ph.D. is comparatively high for Jewish students—23 percent. However, the figures for Protestants and Catholics are similar; if anything the Catholic proportion is higher (15 percent as compared to 12 percent). Among students enrolled in ranking universities and colleges, Catholics have the highest proportion aspiring to obtain a Ph.D. The figures are as follows: Catholics, 30 percent; Protestants, 24 percent; Jews, 24 percent. (The Jewish proportion is somewhat depressed because of the high number planning professional careers that do not involve a Ph.D.) Far from being underrepresented in

---

[3] An early indication of this trend emerged from Andrew Greeley's study based on a 1961 sample of college seniors. Greeley found that Catholics constituted 25 percent of the graduating class and resembled Protestants in their occupational values and career plans. When interviewed a year after graduation, roughly the same proportion of Protestants, Catholics, and Jews planned on getting a Ph.D. (Greeley, 1963, p. 137).

[4] These figures are somewhat inflated because one-quarter of the sample did not answer the question concerning career plans, and are excluded from the percentage base. Also, other students will undoubtedly change their career plans. However, these factors should not distort the comparisons between religious groups.

higher education, in another generation the proportion of Catholics among the nation's faculty may well exceed their national average.

The representation of Jews among faculty has undergone a similar, though less dramatic, increase. Jews were already overrepresented among the oldest cohort of faculty, and the proportion has continued to rise with successive age cohorts, from 5.5 percent to 8.2, 9.5, and 9.6. Among graduate students planning a career in college teaching, the figure is again 9.6 percent. While the overall increase is large, closer examination of the figures indicates that the major increase occurred with the 45–54 age group. In 1945 this group ranged in age from 21 to 30, indicating that Jews made their breakthrough in college teaching immediately after the Second World War. Since then, however, increases between age cohorts have grown steadily smaller. The absolute number of Jewish faculty has increased, but not as fast as the total population of faculty. In this sense the data suggest that Jewish representation among college faculty may be tapering off.[5]

As a matter of simple arithmetic, the increase of Catholics and Jews must involve a decrease of Protestants. Whereas the overwhelming majority—76 percent—of the oldest faculty are Protestant, this has gradually declined to 63 percent among the youngest faculty and to 58 percent among graduate students with academic intentions. Indeed, the Index of Representation (Table 13) shows that, relative to their proportions in the general population, Protestants and Catholics are equally represented among graduate students who plan an academic career. As will be seen in Chapter 6, in some disciplines Protestants are today a bare majority. It is apparent that Protestant dominance of American higher education is becoming a thing of the past.

It is important to examine these trends within the context of institutional quality. If the Catholic increase were characteristic only of lower-ranking institutions, then their greater numbers might not indicate an improvement in academic performance or productivity. Nor would the Protestant decline be as significant.

Table 14 shows the religious distribution by age for the 17

[5] However, Jews have recently broken into college administration for the first time. As Lipset and Ladd (1971, p. 92) report: "Administrative positions were the last to be opened to Jews, but during the late 1960s these restrictions were also broken. Chicago, Cincinnati, Dartmouth, MIT, Pennsylvania, and Rutgers recently appointed Jewish presidents. . . . The first Jewish dean of Harvard Law School, and the first in the university's history, was designated in 1971."

ranking universities. As observed earlier, Catholics are under-represented in these institutions, and this holds true at every age level. However, the proportion of Catholics shows the same increase in the quality institutions as was observed for all institutions together. From the oldest to the youngest age group, the proportion increases from 10 to 11 to 13 to 16 percent, and among graduate students with academic intentions it rises again to 20 percent. In short, while Catholics continue to be underrepresented in the quality institutions, they are rapidly closing the gap, just as in higher education as a whole.

TABLE 14
Religious background by age among faculty in the 17 ranking universities

Religious background	Age of faculty				Graduate students planning a career in college teaching
	55+	45–54	35–44	34—	
Protestant	71.8%	64.1%	56.4%	55.2%	52.0%
Catholic	9.6	10.9	13.3	16.0	20.1
Jewish	12.1	15.7	19.4	18.5	15.8
Other	2.4	3.6	5.0	3.8	5.0
None	4.1	5.7	6.0	6.5	7.2
Number	8,176	11,466	17,209	17,429	145,512
	Index of representation				
Protestant	108	97	85	83	78
Catholic	37	42	52	62	78
Jewish	378	491	606	578	493

On the other hand, the Jewish proportion again shows signs of tapering off. While one cannot place too much confidence in projections based on graduates who say they plan an academic career, it appears that Jewish representation in quality institutions reached its peak in the 35–44 age cohort and has since been on the decline.

Finally, the trend toward diminishing Protestant representation is even more pronounced in the quality institutions than in higher education as a whole. Whereas Protestants constituted 72 percent of faculty in the oldest age cohort, they are a bare majority of young faculty and of graduate students planning a career in college teaching. Those in the Protestant establishment who once resisted the incursions of immigrants would probably see in these trends the realization of their worst fears. In point of fact, American higher education has ceased to be a Protestant institution.

Ordinarily the disproportionate number of Jews in the better institutions is taken as another sign of Jewish academic excellence. However, the issue is not so easily settled. Is attendance at a quality institution a function of the selection of the more able candidates? Or would it be more correct to say that the better institutions produce the better scholars? Let us take graduate students and the observed concentration of Jews in the better graduate schools as an example. Does this indicate superior performance on the part of Jewish students as undergraduates? Or do Jews attend the better schools in greater numbers for some other reasons? A simple explanation might be that, more than others, Jews happen to reside in states where the better schools are located. A second possibility is that Jews more often have the desire and the economic resources to travel to the better schools. A third possibility is that Jews start out in better institutions as undergraduates and that this determines their future career line as graduate students and later as faculty.

The first two hypotheses can be promptly eliminated. The Jewish concentration in the quality institutions cannot be explained in terms of Jewish affluence. There is little or no relation between the quality of an institution and the financial condition of students or their parents. Graduate students in lower-quality institutions are almost as likely to report that their finances are adequate and that their parents are financially well off as students in higher-quality institutions. Graduate schools select out students who can absorb the costs of further education and delayed earnings, and this is as true of lower- as of higher-quality institutions. For the same reason there are only small differences by religion. The percentage saying that their parents were financially comfortable during the time they were growing up is 74 percent for Jews, 72 percent for Protestants, and 68 percent for Catholics. The percentages saying that their current finances are adequate are 78, 77, and 74 percent. Thus despite the fact that in the national population Jews are better off economically than non-Jews, the differences among graduate students are very slight and could not explain the relative concentration of Jews in the ranking institutions.

The proposition that Jewish students are more willing to travel to the better institutions must also be discarded. The data show that the proportion who moved to the state in which their graduate institution is located is the same for all religious groups. Nor can it be said that Jews attend better graduate schools because they happen to live in states where these schools are located. The data show that Jews are more likely to attend quality institutions whether they grew up in the same state or not.

The next question is whether the relatively high representation of Jews in the ranking graduate schools reflects superior academic performance on the part of Jewish students as undergraduates. However imperfect, undergraduate grade-point average is a reasonable indicator of a student's academic performance, and in any event is the one generally used by admissions committees. It might be assumed that Jewish students, given their high representation at the better graduate schools, also have higher undergraduate grades. This is not the case, however (Table 15, item 2). The proportion reporting an undergraduate grade-point average of A is about the same for Jews as for non-Jews (17 versus 19 percent).[6] The overall grade-point average for both groups is 3.0. If grades are any indicator of academic excellence, by this standard Jews do not excel over others.

TABLE 15
Comparisons between Jewish and non-Jewish graduate students on undergraduate grades and institutional background

		Jews	Non-Jews
1.	*Percentage in a ranking university as graduate students*	27	15
2.	*Percentage with an A undergraduate average*	17	19
3.	*Percentage in a ranking university as an undergraduate*	21	10
4.	*Percentage in a ranking college as an undergraduate*	19	3
5.	*Total percentage in a ranking university or college**	40	13
6.	*Percentage with an A undergraduate average among:*		
	a. *Those in a high-ranking undergraduate university*	23	21
	b. *Those in a high-ranking undergraduate college*	14	17
7.	*Percentage attending a ranking university among those having attended:*		
	a. *A high-ranking undergraduate university*	54	47
	b. *A high-ranking undergraduate college*	19	17
8.	*Percentage attending a ranking university standardizing for undergraduate institutional quality*	27	23

* The quality of the undergraduate institution is known only for 45 percent of the sample; the remaining cases are omitted.

[6] Protestants and Catholics are combined in this analysis because they are basically alike on the variables under examination. For example, 20 percent of Protestants report an A undergraduate grade-point average, as compared to 17 percent of Catholics. The proportion who attended a high-ranking university or college is 24 percent in the case of Protestants; 20 percent in the case of Catholics.

It could be argued that Jewish students obtained their grades at higher-quality and more competitive undergraduate colleges, and that therefore their grade-point averages, while nominally the same as those of non-Jews, nevertheless indicate a higher level of excellence. It is true that on the whole Jewish graduate students received their undergraduate education at higher-ranking institutions. The differences are striking: 40 percent of Jewish students came from the highest-ranking colleges and universities, as compared to just 13 percent of non-Jews (Table 15, item 5).[7] However, the important question is how Jews compare to non-Jews in the same institutions. Do they get better grades?

The data indicate that they do not (Table 15, items 6a and 6b). At both high-ranking universities and colleges the difference between Jews and non-Jews in their grade-point averages is negligible. Thus even when compared to non-Jews in institutions of the same rank, Jewish students do not show a tendency to receive higher grades.

Nor are Jewish students in a given institution very much more likely to go on to a high-quality graduate school than non-Jewish students in the same institution who also enter graduate school (Table 15, items 7a and 7b). For example, among graduate students who came from ranking undergraduate universities, 54 percent of Jewish students went on to a ranking university, in comparison to 47 percent of non-Jews. When the relation between religion and quality of graduate school is standardized for the quality of the undergraduate school, the Jewish tendency to attend ranking graduate institutions is no longer pronounced (Table 15, item 8). Put another way, if as many non-Jewish as Jewish graduate students attended quality undergraduate schools, there would be no difference between them in their representation at the quality graduate schools. The overrepresentation of Jews in the better graduate schools seems to be an extension of their overrepresentation in the better undergraduate schools.

Given the intense competition for places in the better undergraduate institutions, the fact that Jews are overrepresented presumably

[7] The quality of the undergraduate institution is known for only 45 percent of the sample. Because of practical considerations, respondents were not asked their undergraduate institution. Instead, they were given a list of 45 of the major Ph.D.-producing institutions. Undergraduate quality is also known if a respondent's undergraduate institution is the same as his graduate institution. Because of this, the descriptive figures in Table 15 (items 3 to 5) are somewhat inflated. However, the comparisons between Jews and non-Jews should not be affected by this problem.

reflects a superior performance in high school. There is also evidence in the undergraduate study that on the whole Jewish students achieve higher grades and more often plan to go to graduate school than do non-Jewish students in the same institutions. For example, in the ranking colleges 37 percent of Jewish students report an A grade-point average, as compared to 20 percent of Protestants and Catholics.[8] The point of the findings reported above, however, is that the self-selective process involved in the decision to go to graduate school appears to place Jewish and non-Jewish students on an equal footing. Thus when Jews and non-Jews in the graduate student population are compared, we find that they are equally likely to have achieved high undergraduate grades and, once the quality of the undergraduate institution is taken into account, to enter a quality graduate school. Put another way, Jewish students enter graduate school with no better qualifications than non-Jewish students from comparable undergraduate institutions.

These findings suggest that there is considerable "tracking" in higher education, in the sense that students who receive their early training in prestigious undergraduate colleges are likely to continue along a prestigious route. This does not mean such students do not develop superior skills and qualifications along the way. But insofar as the difference between Jews and non-Jews is concerned, the crucial factor is that Jews more often begin their academic careers at quality undergraduate institutions. This seems to establish their future path to the better institutions, first as graduate students and later as faculty.

THE PROTESTANT DENOMINATIONS So far in this analysis, Protestants have been examined as a single group. However, we should not overlook the fact that there is a wide assortment of Protestant denominations, different in theology and religious practice, in social outlook, and in the social class and region of their constitutents. At one end of the spectrum are Episcopalians, Presbyterians, and Congregationalists, whose members come largely from the urban East and from the upper strata of education and social class. Studies show that these groups tend to replace traditional religious belief and practice with modern

---

[8] The difference in the ranking universities is less striking. The proportion with an A grade-point average is 13 percent for both Protestants and Catholics, and 18 percent for Jews. In terms of career aspirations, Protestants and Catholics are again alike: 12 percent of Protestants and 15 percent of Catholics said they hoped to get a Ph.D. Among Jews the figure is 23 percent.

interpretations consistent with their education and social class (Stark & Glock, 1968). At the other end of the spectrum are the fundamentalist denominations, especially Southern Baptists and Missouri Lutherans, whose religious commitments are much more traditional. Their members come largely from the lower social strata, and, geographically, from the South and Border States. It is therefore of limited meaning to present figures showing this or that proportion of Protestants in higher education, when these overall figures obscure an uneven representation of the various Protestant denominations. With this in mind, let us examine differences within Protestantism.

Such data are available only for graduate students. While this precludes an analysis of the historical trend among faculty, it does permit an assessment of the contemporary situation among the nation's graduate students and the likely religious distribution among the next generation of faculty.

Table 16 shows three sets of figures: the percentage share of each denomination among the nation's Protestants, the percentage among graduate students, and the percentage among graduate students in ranking universities. In order to avoid blurring denominational effects with those of race, figures are reported for whites only.

Baptists are the largest Protestant denomination, consisting of roughly a quarter of all white Protestants in the nation. However, they are only 16 percent of the nation's graduate students and 10

			Graduate students
Protestant denominations	*Nation**	*All graduate students*	*in ranking universities*
Baptists	24%	16%	10%
Methodists	21	25	21
Lutherans	12	13	11
Presbyterians	10	15	20
Episcopalians	5	9	13
Congregationalists	4	7	8
Other	24	15	17
Number		516,322	82,731

TABLE 16 *Distribution of Protestant denominations in the nation, among graduate students and among graduate students in the ranking universities (whites only)*

* U.S. Bureau of the Census (1958). Estimates for Episcopalians, Congregationalists, and Unitarians are based on a 1964 representative national sample (Selznick & Steinberg, 1964, p. xv).

percent of graduate students in ranking universities. Methodists and Lutherans are represented among graduate students in roughly the same proportions as in the national population. Three denominations are substantially overrepresented among graduate students: Presbyterians, Episcopalians, and Congregationalists. Their representation is even higher in the ranking universities. For example, Episcopalians are only 5 percent of the nation's Protestants, but 9 percent of the Protestant graduate students and 13 percent of Protestants in the ranking universities.[9]

Table 11 showed that among graduate students the ratio of representation for Protestants was 87. It now appears that some Protestant denominations are far less represented than this figure would suggest, while others are heavily overrepresented. For example, the ratio of representation is just 67 for Baptists but 180 for Episcopalians. Like Episcopalians, Presbyterians and Congregationalists are each represented among graduate students in proportions that far exceed their proportions in the national population. Evidently Jews are not the only religious group with a penchant for higher education. However, it is curious that the overrepresentation of Episcopalians is commonly understood to reflect their favorable position in the class system, whereas the overrepresentation of Jews is usually explained in terms of a special value on education with sources in Jewish religion and culture.

RELIGIOUS CONCENTRATIONS WITHIN INSTITUTIONS Most students attend college in the same state or the same region in which they grew up. This proximity factor means that the religious composition of a particular college or university is apt to reflect the religious composition of the state or region in which it is located. Since Catholics and Jews tend to be concentrated in the urban Northeast, one would expect to find large religious concentrations on this account alone.

Nevertheless, the extent of Jewish concentration is still surprising. Of all Jewish graduate students in the sample, 58 percent are

---

[9] Just as the data show Protestant, Catholic, and Jewish graduate students to be alike in terms of their career plans, there are no differences to speak of among Protestant denominations. The proportion who say they expect to pursue a career in college teaching is as follows: Episcopalians, 34 percent; Presbyterians, 37 percent; Congregationalists, 28 percent; Methodists, 35 percent; Lutherans, 28 percent; Baptists, 38 percent; Southern Baptists, 36 percent; Missouri Lutherans, 35 percent. While religious background seems to influence the chances an individual will attend graduate school, it has little or no influence on career plans among those already in graduate school.

found in just 10 institutions. These same 10 institutions account for just 24 percent of all graduate students. Despite this high concentration, in only 3 of 148 institutions in the sample do Jews constitute a majority of the graduate enrollment.

Most of the heavily Jewish institutions are among those with high-quality ratings. Of the 10 institutions with the greatest numbers of Jewish students, 8 are among the 17 ranking universities; only 1 is in the third rank. The concentration of Jews in some of the better institutions perhaps explains the association that is frequently made between Jews and academic prominence.

Although some Catholic colleges and universities are included in our sample, most are very small and account for only a small percentage of all Catholic graduate students. The 10 institutions with the largest concentrations of Catholics account for 37 percent of all Catholic graduate students in the sample. This indicates a high degree of concentration, though less than was observed for Jews. As with Jews, the Catholic concentration is rarely so great as to constitute a numerical majority.

Except for denominational schools, it is rare for any single Protestant denomination to predominate. However, there are some noteworthy denominational differences related to regional and class factors. In some of the elite Eastern colleges Episcopalians, Presbyterians, and Congregationalists are found in disproportionate numbers. On the other hand, many of the institutions in the West and South have heavy concentrations of Protestants from denominations that are theologically and socially more conservative.

Faculty, of course, are more mobile than students, but there is still a good deal of concentration along religious lines. Largely due to the existence of Catholic colleges, 30 percent of all Catholic faculty teach at institutions whose faculties are more than one-half Catholic. On the other hand, one-third teach at institutions that are less than 15 percent Catholic. In other words, Catholics tend to be found at institutions that have either very high or very low Catholic representations.

Although Jews are only 8 percent of all faculty, they tend to be concentrated in a relatively few institutions, just as was observed for graduate students. Indeed, half of all Jewish faculty teach at institutions whose faculties are at least 20 percent Jewish. There are 27 such institutions in the total sample of 303. Such concentrations are bound to give the illusion of greater numbers than is actually the case. As the next chapter shows, religious concentrations within institutions are further highlighted by religious concentrations within academic disciplines.

CONCLUSION   Since the Second World War Catholics have substantially improved their position in the class system. On the basis of national surveys extending from 1943 until 1965, one study reached the following conclusion:

> At the end of World War II, Protestants in the United States ranked well above Catholics in income, occupation, and education; since then Catholics have gained dramatically and have surpassed Protestants in most aspects of status. . . . If the recent trend continues, Catholics in the nation as a whole will surge well ahead of Protestants in all major status variables in the next few years (Glenn & Hyland, 1967, pp. 84–85).

As the study pointed out, one reason for the rapid advancement of Catholics is that they are concentrated "in the larger non-Southern metropolitan areas, where earnings, occupational distributions, educational opportunities, and rates of mobility are more favorable" (ibid., p. 84). Nevertheless, the fact remains that as a group Catholics have overcome many of the social class disabilities which they had as immigrants. The findings reported in this chapter indicate that as Catholics have improved their class position, they have also begun to produce their numerical share of scholars and scientists.

While the Carnegie Commission surveys did not inquire into the ethnic background of respondents, there is good reason to think that certain ethnic groups have contributed disproportionately to the upswing in Catholic representation among college faculty. A national survey of American Catholics found that of all Catholic ethnic groups, Irish have the highest level of educational attainment. In 1963, when the survey was conducted, 77 percent of those whose fathers were Irish had completed high school. The comparable figures for other ethnic groups were as follows: Germans, 62 percent; Italians, 59 percent; Poles, 46 percent; French, 42 percent (Greeley, 1971, p. 67). A 1961 study of college seniors also found that the representation of Irish was twice that of Italians, despite the fact that both groups are about equally represented in the national population (Greeley, 1963, p. 30). Presumably these same ethnic differences would show up among college faculty if comparisons were possible.

6. The Religious Composition of Academic Disciplines

The previous chapter examined the differential tendency of religious groups to enter institutions of higher learning. This chapter is concerned with what they do once they get there. To what extent do Protestants, Catholics, and Jews differ in their choice of academic disciplines? And are these differences as pronounced now as in the past?

THE RELIGIOUS DISTRIBUTION IN ACADEMIC DISCIPLINES: AN OVERVIEW Table 17 orders each of 45 academic disciplines according to their religious composition. For each religious group it shows which fields have average concentrations; which are the most Protestant, Catholic, and Jewish; and which are the least so. An average concentration is defined arbitrarily as within two percentage points on either side of the mean. For example, since Protestants are 66 percent of all faculty, an "average concentration" ranges between 64 and 68 percent. The "most Protestant" fields are at least 69 percent Protestant; the "least Protestant" fields have 63 percent or fewer Protestants.[1]

The most Protestant fields are agriculture, home economics, geography, industrial arts, music, botany, physical and health education, journalism, education, zoology, earth sciences, and dramatics and speech. In each instance Protestants make up over 70 percent of all faculty (Table 17A). Most of these fields disproportionately recruit people from small town and rural backgrounds, and on this basis alone one would expect Protestants to be heavily represented. However, this does not mean that religious values are irrelevant. Because rural America has always

---

[1] This procedure is intended only to highlight fields of heavy and light concentration. Obviously, a five percentage point spread is of greater significance when the mean is 9, as in the case of Jews, than when it is 66, as in the case of Protestants.

TABLE 17A *Protestant representation in academic disciplines*

Academic disciplines	Most Protestant (69% or more)	Average (64–68%)	Least Protestant (63% or less)
Professions			Medicine (58)
			Law (50)
Semiprofessions	Agriculture (94)	Library sciences (67)	Social work (58)
	Home economics (83)	Engineering (64)	
	Industrial arts (78)	Architecture (64)	
	Physical education (76)	Nursing (64)	
	Journalism (74)		
	Education (74)		
	Business (69)		
Physical sciences	Earth sciences (73)	Chemistry (68)	Physics (59)
		Mathematics (65)	
Biological sciences	Botany (77)	Physiology (66)	Biochemistry (56)
	Zoology (74)		Bacteriology (59)
	Biology (69)		
Social sciences	Geography (79)	Anthropology (66)	Sociology (61)
		Political science (64)	Psychology (61)
			Economics (60)
			Experimental psychology (58)
			Social psychology (49)
			Clinical psychology (46)
Fine arts	Music (78)	Art (64)	
	Dramatics and speech (72)	Fine arts (62)	
Humanities		History (65)	Foreign languages (51)
		English (64)	Spanish (50)
		Religion (64)	Philosophy (49)
		German (62)	French (48)

been predominantly Protestant, rural and religious values have interacted over a long period of time, each helping to shape the other. Consequently, it is impossible to separate one from the other. For instance, practicality is an attribute characteristic of rural people regardless of their religion; it is also characteristic (in an ideal-typical sense) of Protestants, whether rural or urban. The important thing to be said here is that all the most Protestant fields, with the exception of music, belong to the practical sciences or

TABLE 17B *Catholic representation in academic disciplines*

Academic disciplines	Most Catholic (21% or more)	Average (16–20%)	Least Catholic (15% or less)
Professions		Law (19)	Medicine (14)
Semiprofessions	Nursing (31)	Industrial arts (19)	Journalism (11)
	Library science (21)	Business (18)	Home economics (10)
		Architecture (18)	Agriculture (9)
		Physical Education (18)	
		Education (17)	
		Social work (17)	
		Engineering (16)	
Physical sciences		Mathematics (19)	Physics (14)
		Chemistry (18)	Earth sciences (13)
Biological sciences		Biology (16)	Bacteriology (14)
			Biochemistry (13)
			Physiology (12)
			Zoology (11)
			Botany (11)
Social sciences		Sociology (18)	Clinical psychology (14)
		Psychology (17)	Geography (13)
		Social psychology (17)	Experimental psychology (13)
		Political science (16)	
		Economics (16)	Anthropology (8)
Fine arts	Art (22)	Fine arts (19)	Dramatics and speech (13)
			Music (11)
Humanities	Spanish (41)		
	Philosophy (36)		
	French (35)		
	Religion (32)		
	Foreign languages (32)		
	German (25)		
	English (22)		
	History (21)		

the vocations. They are fields that tend to deal with practical applications rather than basic research, with the concrete rather than the abstract.

TABLE 17C *Jewish representation in academic disciplines*

Academic disciplines	Most Jewish (12% or more)	Average (7-11%)	Least Jewish (6% or less)
Professions	Law (27)		
	Medicine (23)		
Semiprofessions	Social work (17)	Engineering (10)	Journalism (5)
		Architecture (10)	Education (5)
		Business (8)	Industrial arts (2)
		Library science (7)	Physical Education (2)
			Nursing (1)
			Home economics (1)
			Agriculture (1)
Physical sciences	Physics (14)	Mathematics (8)	Earth sciences (4)
		Chemistry (7)	
Biological sciences	Biochemistry (22)	Zoology (7)	Botany (5)
	Bacteriology (18)	Biology (7)	
	Physiology (12)		
Social sciences	Clinical psychology (36)		Geography (2)
	Experimental psychology (21)		
	Social psychology (20)		
	Economics (16)		
	Psychology (14)		
	Anthropology (13)		
	Sociology (12)		
	Political science (12)		
Fine arts		Dramatics and speech (10)	Art (6)
		Fine arts (9)	Music (6)
Humanities		French (10)	German (5)
		History (9)	Spanish (3)
		Philosophy (9)	Religion (2)
		Foreign languages (8)	
		English (7)	

One of the empirical observations that Weber cited at the outset of *The Protestant Ethic and the Spirit of Capitalism* was that Protestant students tended to be concentrated in technical and commercial studies, whereas Catholics were found disproportionately in the humanities (Weber, 1930, p. 38). What Weber observed for late nineteenth-century Germany is true of the United States today. Catholics continue to be most highly concentrated in the humanities (Table 17B), and the number of Catholics in fields closely related to modern capitalism is relatively small. For example, business, engineering, economics, and political science all have fewer Catholics than do any of the eight disciplines classified under the humanities.

In comparison to Protestants and Jews, Catholics are much more evenly distributed across academic disciplines. Except for the humanities and nursing, there are no fields where the Catholic proportion far exceeds the average among faculty as a whole. In contrast, Protestants and Jews are more clustered, and tend to form mirror images of one another: in fields that are heavily Protestant, there are virtually no Jews; conversely, in fields that are heavily Jewish, Protestant representation is far below average.

As observed earlier, there are proportionately fewer Catholics in the ranking institutions than in higher education as a whole. This is true in most, though not all, disciplines. Exceptions are in medicine, education, Spanish, French, music, and physiology where the proportion of Catholics is almost as great in the ranking institutions as in others. Most other fields show a substantial decline. In mathematics the Catholic proportion declines from 19 to 13 percent; in sociology from 18 to 10; in law from 19 to 14; in English from 22 to 14; in history from 21 to 10; in philosophy from 36 to 14. However, as was also observed earlier, the underrepresentation of Catholics in the ranking institutions is much less marked among the young than among the old, and this is true for each of the disciplines just mentioned.

Although the humanities is the most Catholic field in higher education as a whole, this pattern is not as pronounced in the ranking institutions. There are as many Catholics in medicine, law, engineering, education, and the fine arts as in the humanities. On the other hand, even in the ranking universities there are more Catholics in the humanities than in the physical, biological, or social sciences, or in business.

Jews tend to be either highly represented in a discipline or to be virtually not represented at all (Table 17C). The overrepresentation of Jews is greatest in departments of clinical psychology, followed by law, medicine, biochemistry, experimental psychology, and social psychology. In each of these fields Jews constitute at least 20 percent of all faculty, and in most cases the figures for the quality institutions are even higher. For example, the percentage of Jews on law faculties is 27 percent in all institutions but 36 percent in the ranking universities.

Among the physical sciences, physics has the highest Jewish representation. Jews are 14 percent of physicists and 26 percent of those in the ranking universities. Jews also have a solid representation in mathematics, especially in the better institutions. The figures are 8 and 20 percent. In chemistry and the earth sciences the Jewish representation is comparatively low, especially in the ranking universities.

In the biological sciences Jews tend to be concentrated in those fields with an affinity to medicine: bacteriology, biochemistry, and to a lesser degree, physiology and anatomy. The link between Jews and medicine dates back at least to medieval Europe where, as Lewis Feuer (1963, p. 310) points out, "a young Jew with scientific powers could not realistically aspire to a career in teaching or research at a university laboratory." Undoubtedly patterns of discrimination in American professions and universities have also shaped the pattern of Jewish concentration in academic fields, including changes in this pattern that are examined later in this chapter.

Although Jews have figured prominently among the nation's writers and artists, they are relatively absent among faculties in the humanities and fine arts. In music and art the Jewish proportion is only 6 percent; moreover, the figures are only slightly higher in the quality universities. Although Jews are somewhat better represented in the humanities, these fields are among those with the lowest Jewish concentration. Jews are just 7 percent of faculty in English (13 percent in the better universities). In most foreign languages the Jewish representation is even lower. Indeed, the overall representation of Jews in the fine arts and humanities is no higher than in engineering.

Two exceptions are history and philosophy. Although the proportion of Jews in these fields is about average (9 percent), in the ranking universities Jews are 20 percent of philosophers and 22 percent of historians. It is tempting to speculate that Jews in philosophy and history specialize in areas that bring them close to social science, for example, in ethics rather than metaphysics, and in American rather than European history. However, data to verify this point are not available.

In Table 17 the social sciences, with the exception of psychology, were not among the most heavily Jewish fields. However, the picture in the leading universities is quite different. Here Jews constitute 34 percent of sociology, 28 percent of economics, and 24 percent of political science. The notable exception is anthropology. Jews are 13 percent of all anthropologists, and the figure is no higher in the quality institutions. Anthropology is the most heavily Protestant of the social sciences. In addition, it has the largest proportion of people who report that they were raised without religion. Like most of the social sciences, faculties in social work are heavily Jewish.[2]

At least two qualities seem to characterize the fields in which Jews are most heavily represented. First, they are fields that are people oriented and that, directly or indirectly, are concerned with administering to physical or social ills. This includes medicine, law, clinical psychology, the social sciences, social work, and the medically related biological sciences. A second attribute of "Jewish fields" is that they tend to be abstract and theoretical. There are greater concentrations of Jews in physics and mathematics than in chemistry or earth sciences. Another example is found in engineering: the proportion of Jews in electrical engineering, which is the most theoretical branch of engineering, is much greater than in mechanical, civil, or chemical engineering.

Just as important are the attributes of the fields in which the Jewish representation is comparatively low. If Jews are attracted to the social, they seem to avoid the cultural. Hence Jewish representation is low in the fine arts, most of the humanities, and anthropology. It would not be accurate to say that Jews avoid fields that are directed toward practical rather than scholarly ends, for

[2] Veblen's essay on "The Intellectual Pre-Eminence of Jews in Modern Europe," first written in 1919, is probably the best theory yet advanced to explain the affinity of Jews for social science. Veblen argued that the Jew's marginality and alienation left him with a critical perspective on established institutions and prevailing systems of belief, and made him "a disturber of intellectual peace" (in Lerner, 1948, p. 475). However, such qualities as marginality and alienation are less compatible with the intellectual content and style of the humanities and the fine arts. These are disciplines that traditionally have functioned as repositories of culture, and are likely to recruit individuals with personal and social ties to the cultural past. On the other hand, it could be argued that Jewish marginality and alienation have helped to determine the critical nature of the social and psychological sciences, and will have a similar impact on more conservative disciplines as the representation of Jews increases. Future studies in the sociology of knowledge should explore the subtle interrelationships that exist between the social composition of a discipline and its major intellectual currents.

social work and clinical psychology are among the most Jewish of all fields. However, applied fields that are not people oriented have the lowest concentrations of Jews. The prime example is engineering; other examples are chemistry, the earth sciences, and botany.

One might suppose that given the Jewish penchant for education, Jews would be highly represented in departments of education, but this is not the case. One reason may be that education in the past has not carried much prestige or attracted scholars with high academic qualifications. But this could also be said of social work, which has a high Jewish representation. A more important reason for the small number of Jews in education probably has to do with the historic role of the lower schools in preserving the nation's Protestant heritage. More than almost any other institution in American society, the schools have resisted pressures generated by groups outside the mainstream. Teachers in the lower schools have been disproportionately white and Protestant, from small town and rural backgrounds, and conservative in their social and political outlook. Thus the fact that three-quarters of faculty in education are Protestant is consistent with the generally Protestant character of the nation's school system. At least until recently, the lower schools have not been an avenue of opportunity for Jews and other minorities.

The patterns of religious concentration just observed all have some basis in tradition. Catholics have long been identified with the humanities, Protestants with education and science, Jews with social science and the professions. The next question is whether these traditional patterns are breaking down. Are traditionally Protestant fields still predominantly Protestant among the more recent generations of scholars? Has the Catholic increase in higher education produced a greater representation of Catholics in the physical and social sciences? Are younger Jews entering fields that their predecessors used to avoid because of discrimination or some other factor? Much has been written about the melting-pot tendencies of American society and the gradual disappearance of immigrant cultures. Has this resulted in a tendency for Protestants, Catholics, and Jews to become more alike in their choice of fields, or are differences just as pronounced now as in the past?

RELIGIOUS TRENDS IN ACADEMIC DISCIPLINES Table 18 shows the religious distribution by age for 11 categories of academic disciplines. The bottom section of the table shows the net percentage change for each religious group. In each of the 11 fields the proportion of Protestants has declined between the oldest and youngest groups. The decline has been greatest in law, where the proportion of Protestants has dropped from 70 to 42 percent. It has also been exceptionally large in engineering—from 81 to 59 percent. In none of the 11 categories has the Protestant representation declined by less than 9 percentage points; the average decline for all 11 fields is 15 percentage points.

The Protestant decline has been smallest in the humanities and the fine arts, and in at least one discipline—music—Protestants have nearly maintained their numerical position: the proportion Protestant is 82 percent among the oldest age cohort and 78 percent among the youngest. This is an exception, however. In virtually all other disciplines Protestant representation has dropped off substantially. Indeed, the proportion of Protestants in the *most* Protestant field among the young (education) is roughly the same as the proportion in the *least* Protestant field among the old (the humanities).

Conversely, Catholics have increased their representation in all fields, though to varying degrees. It is greatest in business, engineering, social science, and law, and smallest in medicine, the fine arts, and the humanities. Nevertheless, the humanities continue as the most Catholic field among the young.

Whereas Catholics show a steady increase with successive age cohorts, the trend among Jews is less even. As observed in Chapter 5, Jews made their breakthrough on teaching faculties during the postwar period (with the 45–54 age group), and this pattern shows up again in most fields where Jewish representation has been on the increase. Three exceptions, however, are engineering, law, and medicine. In each case the sharpest Jewish increase occurred a decade later, that is, with the 35–44 age group. This probably reflects the lowering of discriminatory barriers in professional schools during the 1950s.

There is also evidence of a leveling off in Jewish representation in many fields. The proportion of Jews in the physical, biological, and social sciences has barely increased among the youngest three age cohorts. The same is true of the fine arts and the semiprofessions. In all these fields Jewish representation reached its peak, or nearly did so, among the postwar generation of scholars (those between 45 and 54).

Again, medicine and law are notable exceptions. In both fields Jewish representation peaks among the youngest age cohort. Catholics, as we observed, had their smallest increase in the field of tradi-

TABLE 18
The religious
distribution
in academic
disciplines

Academic disciplines	Age			
	55 or older	45–54	35–44	Less than 35
	Percentage Protestants			
Education	82.0	74.9	71.5	69.7
Engineering	80.8	68.8	59.2	59.4
Biological sciences	80.6	67.2	65.9	64.1
Fine arts	80.5	74.2	68.6	68.6
Semiprofessions	80.2	73.7	65.4	68.0
Business	78.9	72.7	65.1	66.0
Physical sciences	76.3	70.1	63.7	63.2
Social sciences	73.3	66.7	62.6	59.0
Law	69.6	47.0	49.0	42.1
Medicine	67.6	62.1	54.6	51.8
Humanities	67.3	62.7	56.5	58.3
	Percentage Catholics			
Education	13.7	16.5	19.1	19.0
Engineering	12.2	15.3	16.9	20.9
Biological sciences	10.2	12.9	14.9	16.5
Fine arts	12.4	12.5	17.7	15.5
Semiprofessions	12.2	15.1	18.2	20.6
Business	8.4	18.3	22.0	19.2
Physical sciences	13.3	14.4	16.6	19.4
Social sciences	11.3	13.2	15.0	20.0
Law	11.1	29.0	14.1	19.0
Medicine	11.2	13.8	15.4	11.4
Humanities	23.8	24.5	27.9	25.8
	Percentage Jews			
Education	2.4	4.7	4.4	6.5
Engineering	2.7	2.7	12.6	9.5
Biological sciences	4.8	11.4	10.8	10.5
Fine arts	3.9	8.8	6.7	8.3
Semiprofessions	4.7	6.3	7.3	5.7
Business	8.9	6.4	7.9	8.3
Physical sciences	5.5	8.4	8.7	8.7
Social sciences	9.7	12.9	13.6	13.4
Law	18.9	16.4	30.8	35.0
Medicine	18.2	19.5	24.0	28.6
Humanities	4.3	6.1	8.0	9.5

Academic disciplines	Age			
	55 or older	45–54	35–44	Less than 35
Net percentage change between the oldest and youngest age cohorts*				
	Protestants		Catholics	Jews
Education	−12.3		+ 5.3	+ 4.1
Engineering	−21.4		+ 8.7	+ 6.8
Biological sciences	−16.5		+ 6.3	+ 5.7
Fine arts	−11.9		+ 3.1	+ 4.4
Semiprofessions	−12.2		+ 8.4	+ 1.0
Business	−12.9		+10.8	− 0.6
Physical sciences	−13.1		+ 6.1	+ 3.2
Social sciences	−14.3		+ 8.7	+ 3.7
Law	−27.5		+ 7.9	+16.1
Medicine	−15.8		+ 0.2	+10.4
Humanities	− 9.0		+ 2.0	+ 5.2

* Figures for Protestants, Catholics, and Jews do not add up to 100 percent because those classified as "other" and "none" are excluded. Together they make up 7 percent of the faculty sample.

tional Catholic concentration—the humanities. Jews did the opposite: they further consolidated their position in the two fields in which historically they have had the strongest foothold.

In only two other fields is Jewish representation at its highest among the youngest cohort of faculty: the humanities and education. To some extent, then, this indicates a breakdown of traditional patterns of concentration. However, in other fields of traditionally low Jewish concentration, there has been little change over time. The most notable examples are departments of music and art where, even among the youngest cohort, Jews constitute only 6 percent of teaching faculty.

On the whole, traditional patterns of religious concentration within academic disciplines have not changed markedly over the past several decades. This can be seen from Table 19, which shows for each age cohort whether there are high, average, or low religious concentrations in various academic fields. For Protestants, Catholics, and Jews alike, the fields that were areas of high or low concentration among the oldest age group remain so among the most recent generation of scholars. Catholics generally are more evenly distributed among the youngest cohort, indicating an increasing tendency for Catholics to enter such fields as the physical and social sciences, but this is an exception to the overall pattern. Thus, de-

spite a general increase of Catholics and Jews in most academic
fields, and a corresponding decrease of Protestants, these trends
have done little to alter the basic pattern of religious concentration
within academic disciplines.

TABLE 19
*Religious
concentrations**
*in academic
disciplines
by age*

Academic disciplines	Age			
	55 or older	45–54	35–44	Less than 35
	Protestants			
Education	H	H	H	H
Fine arts	H	H	H	H
Semiprofessions	H	H	A	H
Business	A	H	A	H
Biological sciences	H	L	A	A
Engineering	H	A	L	L
Physical sciences	A	A	L	A
Social sciences	L	L	L	L
Law	L	L	L	L
Medicine	L	L	L	L
Humanities	L	L	L	L
	Catholics			
Humanities	H	H	H	H
Business	L	A	H	A
Education	A	A	A	A
Semiprofessions	L	A	A	A
Engineering	L	A	L	A
Physical sciences	A	L	L	A
Social sciences	L	L	L	A
Law	L	H	L	A
Fine arts	L	L	A	L
Biological sciences	L	L	L	L
Medicine	L	L	L	L
	Jews			
Law	H	H	H	H
Medicine	H	H	H	H
Social sciences	H	H	H	H
Biological sciences	A	H	A	A
Business	H	A	A	A

TABLE 19
(continued)

Academic disciplines	Age			
	55 or older	45–54	35–44	Less than 35
	Jews (cont.)			
Physical sciences	A	A	A	A
Engineering	L	L	H	A
Fine arts	A	A	L	A
Humanities	A	L	A	A
Semiprofessions	A	A	L	L
Education	L	L	L	L

*H = High; A = Average; L = Low. An average concentration is defined as within two percentage points on either side of the mean for the particular age group. High and low concentrations are above or below this middle range.

THE WAVE OF THE FUTURE: GRADUATE STUDENTS

On the whole, the graduate student data suggest that the trends observed for faculty will continue into the foreseeable future. This can be seen from Table 20, which compares the religious mix of young faculty with that of graduate students who plan a career in college teaching. Earlier we found that in every field the proportion of Catholics increased between oldest and youngest faculty. Table 20 now shows that in most fields the Catholic proportion again increases among graduate students planning an academic career.

TABLE 20 *Religious representation in academic disciplines among young faculty and graduate students who plan a career in college teaching*

	Protestant		Catholic		Jewish	
	Young faculty*	Graduate students†	Young faculty	Graduate students	Young faculty	Graduate students
Physical sciences	63.2%	56.6%	19.4%	20.6%	8.7%	9.1%
Biological sciences	64.1	61.3	16.5	21.1	10.5	9.0
Social sciences	59.0	49.9	20.0	24.5	13.4	13.8
Humanities	58.3	55.9	25.8	24.5	9.5	9.3
Fine arts	68.6	75.1	15.5	13.8	8.3	7.8
Medicine	51.8	47.5	11.4	15.6	28.6	27.0
Law	42.1	40.1	19.0	33.4	35.0	22.8
Engineering	59.4	43.3	20.9	17.0	9.5	5.8
Education	69.7	69.2	19.0	19.7	6.5	7.6
Business	66.0	52.9	19.2	30.3	8.3	9.7
Semiprofessions	68.0	68.5	20.6	18.1	5.7	5.6
TOTAL	62.6%	57.8%	20.5%	22.2%	9.6%	9.6%

*Less than 35 years of age.
† Only graduate students who plan a career in college teaching are included.

Once again, the humanities is an exception. As with faculty, the proportion of Catholics has tapered off as younger Catholic scholars enter other disciplines.

Earlier we also observed a leveling-off pattern among Jews in most academic disciplines. This finding is again confirmed in Table 20. Since the early 1960s, college attendance has been practically universal among Jews of college age. According to one report, 80 percent of Jews of college age are currently enrolled in college, as compared to 40 percent for the population as a whole ("The American Jew Today," 1971, p. 63). Given this fact, together with the steady growth of American higher education, it becomes almost inevitable that the extent of Jewish representation will either stabilize or drop off. Future increases are likely to come from Catholics and from some of the Protestant denominations that continue to be underrepresented.

7. Religious Commitment and Scholarly Productivity

Two different views of the relation between religion and science have been prominent in the sociological tradition. The first stresses areas of compatibility between the ethos of certain religious groups and the requirements of science. The second argues that there is an essential incompatibility between religious and scientific perspectives. That both views are grounded in solid empirical evidence should indicate that the contradictions are more apparent than real. Indeed, a closer examination of these two views suggests a basis for their reconciliation.

In his essay on "Puritanism, Pietism, and Science," Robert Merton (1963) examines elements of early Protestantism that were favorable to the development of science. Like Weber, Merton focuses on value orientations embodied in seventeenth-century Puritanism in England and America and Pietism in Germany. Unlike traditional Catholicism, these sects exalted reason, chiefly as a means for controlling the passions, and encouraged participation in worldly affairs. These orientations were compatible with basic attributes of science, especially its rational empiricism and its utilitarianism. Indeed, the link between religious ideology and science was frequently direct. Early Puritans specifically sanctioned the empirical study of nature. Instead of fearing that science would undermine faith, they viewed it as a means for understanding the wonders of God's creation and for exercising control over a corrupt world. In addition, Protestant injunctions concerning the virtues of discipline, methodic labor, and constant diligence in one's calling produced in individuals a temperament and a disposition that encouraged the pursuit of science.

Like Weber, Merton is careful not to make unlimited claims about the historical significance of the Protestant ethic. Although this ethic was a radical departure from traditional Catholicism and became a historical force in its own right, it was also a product of social trends and ideological currents of the seventeenth century. At best, the Protestant ethic was only one element in the evolution of science. Its main contribution, according to Merton, was that it canonized the essential elements of the scientific spirit. In doing so, it "made an empirically-founded science commendable rather than, as in the medieval period, reprehensible or at best acceptable on sufferance" (Merton, 1963, p. 579).

Merton bolsters his thesis with evidence showing that Protestants in late nineteenth-century Germany and Austria were far more likely than Catholics to pursue scientific and technical studies. From a historical standpoint, there was an essential compatibility between ascetic Protestantism and science.

A second tradition in sociology regards religion and science as fundamentally in conflict. In the spirit of the Enlightenment, Auguste Comte regarded Christianity as an outmoded system of beliefs that was destined to be replaced by positivism, a kind of secular religion that would be faithful to the rational tenets of science. Freud advanced the positivist tradition one step further. In his view (1962) religion resembled an infantile neurosis by creating the comforting illusion of an all-powerful and benevolent father. Just as the reality principle was the psychological ideal for the individual, Freud believed that a sophisticated civilization would reject all religious conceptions that evolved from man's individual and collective infancy. The hallmark of the positivist view is that it sees religion as essentially a relic from the past ultimately to be replaced by the secular ideologies of a scientific age.

Emile Durkheim (1958) was less confident of the outcome of the historic struggle between religion and science. He believed that the integrative functions of religion, both as symbol and as ritual, were too essential to the social fabric to be so easily negated. Durkheim would not deny that the individualism and free thought characteristic of Protestantism served the needs of science or any rational discipline. But he argued that such attributes were destructive of the social bond, and he found proof of this in the high rate of egoistic suicide among Protestants. Implicit in this analysis is a subtle view of the conflict between religion and science: Protestantism may have given rise to science, but in the end science would turn its back on all religion.

Evidence supporting the incompatibility thesis is found in empirical studies of religious patterns in higher education. Prominent among these is Charles Y. Glock and Rodney Stark's analysis of data based on a 1963 sample of the nation's graduate students (1965, Ch. 14). Their findings showed that the rate of apostasy in the student population far exceeded the rate for the population at large. Whereas surveys report that only 3 to 5 percent of American adults claim no religious affiliation, the figure for graduate students was 26 percent. Apostasy was even more common in the higher-ranking colleges and universities. Finally, the data showed that students with more developed scholarly interests were far less likely to have strong religious commitments. Glock and Stark's conclusion was that "religion and scholarship tend to be mutually exclusive perspectives" (1965, p. 283). Another investigator analyzing the same data suggested that in the intellectual community the canons of science and rational inquiry become a functional alternative for religion (Zelan, 1968).

One obvious difference between these two views of the relation between religion and science is that one is historical, the other contemporary. It is possible that in the seventeenth century Protestantism was conducive to science but is no longer so today. Writers frequently fail to distinguish between factors that account for the origin of a phenomenon, and those that account for its perpetuation at a later point in time. Even if the scientific spirit originally sprung from certain religious values, it has clearly been removed from a religious context in modern society. As Weber (1955, pp. 181–182) wrote with respect to the religious foundations of capitalism: "Today the spirit of religious asceticism . . . has escaped from the cage. But victorious capitalism, since it rests on mechanical foundations, needs its support no longer."

There is a still more important difference between the two views discussed above. Merton's observations concern an affinity between a religious *ethos* and certain aspects of science, whereas contemporary studies demonstrating an incompatibility between religion and science are based on *individual* data. For this reason the two sets of findings are not necessarily in contradiction. Even if the Protestant ethic was (or is) conducive to science, it does not necessarily follow that those Protestants with deepest religious commitments will be the ones most apt to act out their secular implications. On the contrary, one suspects that even in the seventeenth century it was not the most deeply involved Puritans but their less pious coreligionists who entered the ranks of science.

There is nothing in Merton's study either to confirm or disconfirm such an interpretation. Merton at one point weighs the difference between group data and individual data: "Of course, the mere fact that an individual is nominally a Catholic or a Protestant has no bearing upon his attitude toward science. It is only as he adopts the tenets and implications of the teachings that his religious affiliation becomes significant" (Merton, 1963, p. 587). However, Merton has no data on the religious beliefs of early scientists. His conclusions were based on data showing that Protestants were more likely than Catholics to enter programs in science. But there is nothing to indicate that it was the more religiously involved Protestants who did so.

In their study of the *Origins of American Scientists,* R. H. Knapp and H. B. Goodrich (1952, p. 275) speculate that what was significant about the Protestant ethic was not its religious qualities but rather its secularism. They write:

. . . Protestantism has been more prone to secularization than Catholicism, and secularization of values permits the development of science. According to this view, Protestant groups and Protestant institutions have produced more scientists because Protestants have more readily abandoned their fundamentalist religious outlook and thus have been freer to accept the tenets of scientific philosophy. But it does not necessarily follow that the doctrines of Protestantism as such are more compatible with science than the doctrines of Catholicism.

If this assumption is correct, and it is the secular tendencies within Protestantism that are the basis of its compatibility with science, then one would expect the scientific spirit to be more often found among Protestants who were marginally religious rather than among their more devout coreligionists.

In short, the two theories of the relation between religion and science are not in fundamental conflict. The compatibility thesis may be correct in stressing an affinity between certain religious values and the scientific spirit and the role that these values played in the historical development of science. And the incompatibility thesis may be correct in its claim that on an individual level religious involvement tends to be inimical to science and other scholarly concerns.

This chapter is primarily concerned with testing the second of these theoretical positions. The focus is on the individual, particularly the relation between his religious commitment and scholarly orientations. The data are drawn from the faculty survey, and the analysis is divided into two parts. The first section assesses the nature and extent of religious commitment among faculty, taking into account institutional quality and academic discipline. The second section analyzes the consequences of religious commitment for scholarly orientations and research productivity.

Table 21 reports the distribution of responses to four questions pertaining to religious commitment that were included in the faculty survey. The first was worded as follows: "I think of myself as (1) deeply religious, (2) moderately religious, (3) indifferent to religion, (4) opposed to religion." In the sample as a whole only 8 percent placed themselves in the extreme category of being opposed to religion. Another 28 percent said they are indifferent to religion. On the other hand, 48 percent indicated they are moderately religious and 16 percent said deeply religious. Depending upon the standard of comparison used, one could either emphasize that two-thirds of all faculty appear to have conventional religious attachments or that one-third lack even minimal religious ties. The more important point, however, is that these proportions vary systematically with such factors as institutional quality, academic discipline, and age, as will presently be seen.

TABLE 21
Religious commitment by religious background

Questions on religious commitment	Religious background			
	Protestants	*Catholics*	*Jews*	*Total**
I consider myself:				
Deeply religious	16%	23%	5%	16%
Moderately religious	52	52	28	48
Indifferent to religion	26	19	50	28
Opposed to religion	6	6	17	8
Would you describe yourself as conservative in your religious beliefs?				
Yes	43	42	19	40
Church attendance:				
Once a week	33	62	5	25
Once a month	49	67	10	48
Present affiliation:				
None	20	19	26	22

* Includes those whose religious background was "other" or "none."

The responses of Protestants and Catholics are notably similar. The proportion saying they are indifferent or opposed to religion is 32 percent for Protestants and 25 percent for Catholics. In sharp contrast, the figure for Jewish faculty is twice as great—67 percent. This is a large difference that could have far-reaching implications if the incompatibility theory of the relation between religious commitment and scholarship should prove correct.

Even a person who characterizes himself as "deeply religious" does not necessarily adhere to traditional tenets of faith. Thus, a second question asked respondents whether or not they are conservative in their religious beliefs. Again, Protestants and Catholics responded similarly: 43 percent of the former and 42 percent of the latter said their religious beliefs were generally conservative. The figure for Jews is just 19 percent.

A third question inquired into the frequency of church attendance. On this item Protestants and Catholics are quite different. Among Catholic faculty 62 percent attend church once a week, as compared to 33 percent of Protestants and just 5 percent of Jews. The comparatively high rate of church attendance among Catholics is customarily taken as a sign of Catholic piety. However, as we have just seen, Catholic faculty are only slightly more likely than Protestants to see themselves as deeply or moderately religious, or as conservative in their religious beliefs. In other words, the greater church attendance of Catholic faculty may not involve greater religious conviction.

After being queried about the religion in which they were raised, respondents were asked about their present religious affiliation. Twenty-two percent of all faculty indicated "none." This, of course, far exceeds the level of nonaffiliation in the general population. Most national surveys report that the proportion claiming no religion is approximately 5 percent.

The proportion of faculty claiming no current affiliation is virtually the same for Catholics (19 percent) as for Protestants (20 percent), and is only slightly higher for Jews (26 percent). Thus, although 67 percent of Jewish faculty indicate they are indifferent or opposed to religion, only 26 percent go so far as to deny any current religious identification. Put another way, among Jewish faculty who said they were indifferent or opposed to religion, only 39 percent do not still identify as Jews. Clearly this reflects the ethnic character of Judaism, and the tendency of Jews to identify as a people as well as a religion.

In contrast, among Protestants and Catholics loss of faith more often involves a total rejection of religious labels. Thus among Protestants who said they were indifferent or opposed to religion, 59 percent report no current affiliation; the comparable figure for Catholics is 63 percent.

The above four measures tap different dimensions of religious commitment and form the basis for constructing a typology that will facilitate more intensive analysis. The pivotal distinction is between those who are deeply or moderately religious and those indifferent or opposed to religion. Among the first group we can further distinguish between those whose religious beliefs are and are not conservative. The second group—those indifferent or opposed to religion—can also be divided between those who retain a nominal religious affiliation and those who renounce all religious ties. Cross-classifying these three items produces eight types, as shown in the diagram below.

| | | *Current religious affiliation?* | |
		Yes	*No*
Deeply or moderately religious	Conservative	Traditionalists	Near-zero cell
	Not conservative	Modernists	Near-zero cell
Indifferent or opposed to religion	Conservative	Near-zero cell	Near-zero cell
	Not conservative	Ethnics	Dropouts

Because of a high consistency of responses, 94 percent of the sample are located in just four cells, each of which represents a conceptually distinct type:

1 *Traditionalists:* Those who have a current religious affiliation and indicate both that they are deeply or moderately religious and conservative in their religious beliefs. As Table 22 shows, 42 percent of both Protestants and Catholics meet all three criteria of religious involvement. In contrast, only 15 percent of Jews do so.

2 *Modernists:* Like the traditionalists, modernists hold a nominal affiliation and are intensely or moderately religious, but they do not describe their religious beliefs as conservative. This combination of responses is characteristic of 29 percent of Protestants, 36 percent of Catholics, and 18 percent of Jews.

TABLE 22 *Religiosity by religious background (ranking universities and all institutions)*

	Ranking universities			All institutions		
Religiosity	Protestants	Catholics	Jews	Protestants	Catholics	Jews
Traditionalists	26%	33%	13%	42%	42%	15%
Modernists	26	28	15	29	36	18
Ethnics	16	8	42	11	6	40
Dropouts	32	31	30	18	16	27
Number*	28,490	6,253	8,214	255,506	72,167	33,496

* In this and subsequent tables, respondents who could not be classified on the typology of religiosity are excluded. Six percent of the sample had anomalous response patterns and seven percent did not answer all three of the component questions.

3   *Ethnics:* Those who say they are indifferent or opposed to religion, and unconservative in their religious beliefs, but who retain a nominal religious identity. This response pattern is practically unique to Jews. Among Jewish faculty, 40 percent score as ethnics, as compared to just 11 percent of Protestants and 6 percent of Catholics.

4   *Dropouts:* Those who give nonreligious responses to all three questions. Unlike the ethnics, they renounce even nominal religious ties. Among faculty as a whole, 21 percent fall into this category. The proportion is highest among those raised as Jews — 27 percent. In the case of Protestants it is 18 percent; in the case of Catholics, 16 percent.

From past research it can be expected that traditionalists and dropouts will be quite different in terms of such variables as academic achievement and political conservatism. Far less certain is how modernists and ethnics will appear. Will modernists resemble the traditionalists, since they share with them strong ties to religion? Or will the fact that their religious beliefs are not of a conservative kind mitigate or neutralize the effect of religious involvement? Similarly, will Jews classified as ethnics be closer to traditionalists or to dropouts in terms of their secular behavior? These questions are addressed presently. The analysis immediately following explores variations in religious commitment by institutional quality and academic discipline. For purposes of this analysis it will be convenient to combine ethnics and dropouts into a single group which will be referred to as *apostates.* Operationally, apostasy is defined as being indifferent or opposed to religion, whether or not this involves a rejection of nominal religious ties.

INSTITUTIONAL VARIATIONS IN RELIGIOUS COMMITMENT   Table 23 shows how apostasy varies with the quality rating of institutions. The direction of the relationship is clear: the higher the rank of the institution, the greater is the proportion of faculty who are indifferent or opposed to religion. Among the 17 ranking universities the rate of apostasy is 54 percent. Among the lowest-ranking colleges it is 22 percent.

For Protestants, Catholics, and Jews alike, apostasy increases with institutional quality. However, among Jewish faculty the level of apostasy is consistently higher and shows less variation. Even among Jews in the lowest-ranking colleges the rate of apostasy is 56 percent. Indeed, the rate of apostasy for Jews in the *lowest*-ranking colleges is higher than the rates for Protestants and Catholics in the *highest*-ranking universities. This finding may provide one clue to the Jewish success in American higher education. If religious involvement is an impediment to scholarly productivity, then the lower level of religious involvement of Jewish scholars might account for some of their success relative to non-Jews.

More is involved than this, however, for even when Jews have relatively strong religious commitments they are almost as likely to reach a ranking university. This is shown in Table 24, which rotates the variables in Table 23 so that religiosity is now an independent variable and institutional quality the dependent variable. Among Protestants and Catholics those with stronger religious commitments are less likely to be in a ranking university. Among Protestants classified as traditionalists only 11 percent are found in ranking institutions, whereas the figure rises to 27 percent among those classified as dropouts. In the case of Catholics the figures are 11 and 24 percent. Among Jewish faculty the differences are much smaller. Traditionalists are almost as likely as dropouts to be in a ranking university: the figures are 29 and 37 percent. In short, religiosity among Jewish faculty does not appear to be a handicap in climbing the academic ladder.

This analysis suggests that in matters of religion Jews have two advantages over non-Jews. First, non-Jews exhibit a pattern of greater religious involvement which is inversely related to academic success. Second, even when Jews do have strong religious commitments they do not experience the same adverse effects that religiosity appears to have among non-Jews. Both these factors undoubtedly help to explain the historic overrepresentation of Jews in the better institutions, though they by no means constitute a complete explanation.

Table 24 has another implication concerning the broad historical trend. It shows that as religious commitment goes from strong to weak, there is a steady decrease in the *difference* between Jews

TABLE 23
Apostasy by
religious
background and
institutional
quality*

Institutional quality	Religious background			
	Protestants		Catholics	
	Percentage	Number	Percentage	Number
Universities				
High	48	28,490	39	6,253
Medium	37	43,926	29	10,333
Low	28	42,554	24	10,245
Colleges				
High	39	14,073	36	2,990
Medium	24	28,726	16	9,859
Low	20	58,893	15	21,190
Junior colleges	20	38,873	18	11,295
TOTAL	29	255,506	22	72,167

* *Apostates* are defined as respondents who describe themselves as indifferent or opposed to religion.

TABLE 24
*Institutional
quality by
religious
background
and religiosity*

Religiosity	Religious background			
	Protestants	Catholics	Jews	Protestant-Jewish difference
	Percentage in a ranking college or university			
Traditionalists	11	11	29	18
Modernists	15	10	28	13
Ethnics	23	16	35	12
Dropouts	27	24	37	10
TOTAL	17	13	34	17
	Numbers			
Traditionalists	106,006	30,061	5,206	
Modernists	75,394	26,133	6,084	
Ethnics	27,495	4,037	13,295	
Dropouts	46,611	11,896	8,911	
Other	31,241	8,178	4,067	
TOTAL	286,745	80,345	37,563	

Jews		Total	
Percentage	*Number*	*Percentage*	*Number*
72	8,214	54	47,760
71	10,369	43	70,132
60	4,474	32	61,617
66	2,884	44	21,916
61	2,716	25	43,199
56	2,976	22	88,458
53	1,863	22	55,456
66	33,496	33	388,538

and non-Jews in terms of representation in a ranking college or university (see last column of Table 24). For example, among traditionalists there is an 18 percentage point difference between Protestants and Jews, but among dropouts it is reduced to 10 percentage points. In other words, if the religious commitments of non-Jews are over time becoming more like those of Jews, then this may help close the gap between Jews and non-Jews in terms of representation in ranking institutions.

TRENDS IN RELIGIOUS COMMITMENT Two questions arise with respect to trends in religious commitment. Are younger faculty less bound to religion than their older colleagues? And if so, are differences between Jews and non-Jews gradually diminishing, or are they as pronounced among the young as among the old?

As Table 25 shows, Protestants, Catholics, and Jews all have experienced a decline in religiosity. In each case the proportion of traditionalists steadily decreases with younger age. The decline has been sharpest among Catholics where the proportion of traditionalists is 64 percent among the oldest age cohort, and then drops off to 52, 39, and 31 percent. While Catholics start out as having more traditionalists than Protestants, they end up in the youngest age cohort with slightly fewer.

Although the proportion of traditionalists has dropped off among all religious groups, the shift has taken different forms. In the case

TABLE 25
Religiosity
by religious
background
and age

Religious	Age			
background	55+	45–54	35–44	34–
Protestants				
Traditionalists	54%	49%	38%	33%
Modernists	27	28	31	30
Ethnics	8	9	12	12
Dropouts	11	14	19	25
Number	41,452	58,522	77,198	77,789
Catholics				
Traditionalists	64%	52%	39%	31%
Modernists	25	32	39	40
Ethnics	3	4	6	7
Dropouts	8	12	16	22
Number	8,302	14,726	23,378	25,582
Jews				
Traditionalists	23%	17%	16%	13%
Modernists	18	19	18	17
Ethnics	35	38	39	43
Dropouts	24	26	27	27
Number	2,876	7,092	11,487	11,962

of Catholics there has been a sharp increase in the number of modernists (those who say they are deeply or moderately religious but whose beliefs are not of a conservative kind). In addition, there is a sharp increase in the proportion of dropouts — from 8 to 22 percent.

Among Protestants the decline of traditionalists has only produced an incidental rise in the proportion of modernists. Most of the change is accounted for by a sharp increase in the proportion of dropouts — from 11 to 25 percent. In contrast, the proportion of dropouts has barely increased among Jews; most of the decrease in traditionalists is offset by an increase in the proportion of ethnics — from 35 to 43 percent.

If one examined only the figures on religious dropouts, they would suggest a pattern of diminishing religious differences in religiosity. Among the oldest group of faculty the proportion of religious dropouts is much higher for Jews (24 percent) than for Protestants (11 percent) or for Catholics (8 percent). But among the youngest faculty this 16 percentage point difference is reduced to just 5. In other words, at the present time each religious group appears to be producing an almost equal number of religious dropouts. However, this is offset by the fact that Jews have always produced a higher proportion of ethnics — those whose religious ties are purely secular — and this proportion has increased over time. Thus, if one combines dropouts with ethnics the differences between Jews and non-Jews are almost as great among the young as among the old.

In general, the data indicate that Catholic faculty have become more like Protestants in their religious commitments, but both groups continue to exhibit much higher rates of religious involvement than Jews. However, these differences are not quite as large among the young as among the old, and they will probably decrease at an even faster rate in the future. Among Jews the proportion of dropouts has leveled off, and since 67 percent presently are either ethnics or dropouts, Jews are bound to reach a threshold where further erosion of religious commitment will be difficult. On the other hand, religiosity is rapidly declining among Protestants and Catholics, and this trend is likely to continue into the future.

It could be argued that Table 25 does not indicate generational change but only the effect of increasing age. According to this interpretation, as younger faculty grow older many will return to the religious fold and eventually exhibit a pattern of religious commitment similar to that of the present-day old. Without panel data this possibility cannot be discounted. However, given what is known about the trend toward secularization in contemporary society and particularly in institutions of higher learning, it is more plausible that younger faculty are simply less steeped in religious values, and are likely to remain so as they grow older.

RELIGIOSITY AND ACADEMIC DISCIPLINE Table 26 shows the rates of apostasy among faculty in 11 academic fields. The left half of the table refers to the 17 ranking universities, the right half to all institutions combined. While many of the details of Table 26 warrant closer inspection, three general patterns emerge:

1 In every field except medicine, the rates of apostasy are substantially higher in the ranking universities than in higher education as a whole.

2 The applied fields generally exhibit significantly lower rates of apostasy than do the more theoretical and intellectual disciplines. Thus apostasy is lowest among faculties in education, the semi-professions, business, and engineering. It is highest in the social sciences, the humanities, the bio-

Academic disciplines	Protestants		Catholics		Jews	
	Percentage	Number	Percentage	Number	Percentage	Number
Education	36	1,885	21	344	60	272
Semiprofessions	36	3,770	30	928	65	897
Business	47	1,699	29	283	62	348
Engineering	39	2,610	28	541	73	549
Fine arts	45	1,504	32	358	67	223
Physical sciences	61	3,174	43	642	81	996
Biological sciences	56	2,572	55	491	80	692
Medicine	33	3,098	24	782	63	1,247
Humanities	53	4,330	51	1,182	75	1,075
Law	71	409	†	†	83	376
Social sciences	66	3,206	66	498	79	1,550

Ranking universities

* *Apostates* are defined as respondents who describe themselves as indifferent or opposed to religion.

† Too few cases for stable percentages.

logical sciences, and the physical sciences. Apostasy is also generally high among faculties of medicine and law. These patterns are basically the same for Protestants, Catholics, and Jews alike.

3 The third major pattern in Table 26 is that the differences in apostasy among Protestants, Catholics, and Jews generally stand up within academic disciplines. In every instance, the rate of apostasy for Jews far exceeds those of Protestants or Catholics, and in most cases Protestants continue to have a higher rate of apostasy than Catholics. This is true both in ranking universities and institutions of lower quality. One notable exception is the humanities: in the ranking universities the level of apostasy for Catholics is just as great as for Protestants. Although the humanities is the most Catholic of all disciplines, it is evidently not the more devout Catholics who are likely to achieve a position in a ranking university.

In short, each of the factors analyzed in Table 26—religion, academic discipline, and institutional quality—influence the rate of apostasy and do so fairly independently of each other. Thus, the high rate of Jewish apostasy cannot be explained simply by the fact that Jews are concentrated in the better institutions or in academic disciplines that are generally high in apostasy. Nor can the low rate of apostasy in certain disciplines or in quality institutions be explained by the relative absence of Jews. Because religion, institu-

		All institutions							
Total		Protestants		Catholics		Jews		Total	
Percentage	Number	Percentage	Number	Percentage	Number	Percentage	Number	Percentage	Number
38	2,642	16	33,206	12	8,033	58	2,109	18	45,269
41	6,030	18	30,441	15	7,303	58	2,569	21	43,159
47	2,494	20	15,182	13	4,206	44	1,656	21	22,294
45	4,028	23	15,499	19	4,208	61	2,237	29	24,201
48	2,299	28	21,125	28	4,227	63	2,230	33	29,371
65	5,508	32	33,800	25	8,664	69	4,217	37	51,204
62	4,219	38	16,823	24	3,683	75	2,651	41	25,389
42	5,510	36	7,249	24	1,795	68	2,897	43	12,713
58	7,607	36	46,085	24	19,899	65	5,687	46	76,807
68	939	43	1,359	20	532	70	779	48	2,853
72	5,926	44	29,643	35	7,751	77	6,243	49	47,399

tional quality, and discipline each has an independent effect on apostasy, the rate of apostasy ranges from 7 percent among Catholic faculty in education in the lowest-ranking colleges to 77 percent among Jewish social scientists in the ranking universities.

Earlier we observed a general decline in religiosity between older and younger faculty. Not all academic fields, however, are part of this overall trend. Among those that do not show a decline in religiosity are business, the semiprofessions, engineering, and medicine. These fields have traditionally attracted people with strong religious inclinations, and this is just as true now as in previous generations. On the other hand, the proportion of apostates has steadily increased in education, the fine arts, the humanities, and the physical and social sciences. Inasmuch as apostasy correlates highly with such factors as scholarly productivity and political liberalism, it is likely that the decline of religiosity is indicative of a broader transformation in the intellectual and political climate within these disciplines.

RELIGION AND SCHOLARSHIP Indirectly, the findings reported above already suggest a connection between religiosity and low scholarly productivity. We observed that the rates of apostasy vary with institutional quality, and reach their highest levels in the more intellectual disciplines. However, institutional quality and academic discipline are contextual variables, and as such they fall short of demonstrating a direct link between an individual's religious commitments and his achievements as a scholar. With this in mind, let us now introduce measures of individual scholarship into the analysis.

Three such measures are used. The first deals with the individual's self-conception, as measured by responses to the statement: "I consider myself an intellectual." The second measures his orientation toward research. Respondents were asked whether their interests lie primarily in teaching or research, and were offered four response categories designating varying degrees of commitment to one or the other. A third measure deals with research activity, as indicated by the number of publications during the two years preceding the survey. These three items are not simply repetitive, but tap different dimensions of scholarship—self-concept, general orientation, and actual behavior.

Table 27 shows the breakdown of responses, controlling for the religion in which faculty were raised. Once again, there is no evidence of a special aversion to scholarship among Catholic faculty, at least as compared to Protestants. The responses to all three items are virtually identical for both groups. However, in each instance Jewish faculty are far more likely than either Protestants or Catholics to respond in ways that indicate a strong commitment to scholarship. The measure of research activity—which is perhaps the most trustworthy of the three measures since it deals with actual behavior—also shows the largest difference. Only 30 percent of Jewish faculty report that they did not have any professional publications in the previous two-year period. In contrast, the figure for Protestants is 55 percent; for Catholics it is 59 percent.

Given the Jewish concentration in the high-ranking, research-oriented universities, it is not surprising that they publish with greater regularity. On the other hand, the fact that Jews are more often oriented to research and productive as scholars helps to account for their representation in quality universities in the first place. Without panel data it is not possible to unravel the causal sequence between these variables. However, it *is* possible to control for institutional quality in order to find out whether Jews continue to exhibit strong orientations toward research even after this factor is taken into account.

This is done in Table 28. Each of the three dimensions of scholarly orientation is strongly a function of institutional quality. For

TABLE 27
Scholarly orientations by religious background

Scholarly orientations	Religious background		
	Protestants	*Catholics*	*Jews*
I consider myself an intellectual:			
Strongly agree	16%	18%	36%
Agree with reservations	52	50	46
Disagree with reservations	24	24	14
Strongly disagree	8	8	4
Research orientation:			
Very heavily in research	3	3	8
In both, but leaning toward research	18	17	35
In both, but leaning toward teaching	34	33	33
Very heavily in teaching	45	47	24
Publications in last two years:			
None	55	59	30
1–2	24	23	27
3–4	12	10	21
5–10	7	6	17
More than 10	2	2	5

TABLE 28
Scholarly orientations by religious background and institutional quality*

Religious background	Universities			Colleges			Junior colleges	Total
	High	*Medium*	*Low*	*High*	*Medium*	*Low*		
Percentage of self-identified intellectuals								
Protestants	25	20	15	22	15	14	10	16
Catholics	29	22	19	27	20	16	8	18
Jews	42	36	30	38	36	32	25	36
Percentage who prefer research								
Protestants	46	37	25	22	11	9	4	21
Catholics	48	36	27	24	13	10	6	20
Jews	58	52	38	40	17	21	17	43
Percentage with 3 or more publications								
Protestants	49	39	26	21	11	7	2	21
Catholics	46	37	24	19	11	7	4	18
Jews	62	54	38	34	17	15	12	44

* The raw numbers can be found in Table 23.

example, among Jewish faculty in the ranking universities 62 percent report three or more publications in the last two years. This declines to 54 and 38 percent in lower-ranking universities, and to 15 percent in the lowest-ranking colleges.

To some extent the better publishing record of Jewish scholars simply reflects their greater concentration in the higher-quality institutions. Within any single category of institutional quality, religious differences are not as great as in the sample as a whole (last column). Nevertheless, religion continues to have a pronounced effect. The publishing record of Jews in medium-ranking universities is as great as that of non-Jews in high-ranking universities; similarly, the Jewish rate in low-ranking universities matches that of non-Jews in medium-ranking universities. Thus in terms of the sheer number of publications, Jewish scholars surpass the record of their non-Jewish colleagues in the same institutions and do as well as non-Jews in institutions of the next highest rank.

Of course, the number of publications is only a superficial measure of scholarship. It says nothing about their quality or about the other criteria that enter into the selection of faculty for the higher-ranking institutions. At least there is nothing in Table 28 to suggest that there are more Jews with active publishing records in lower-ranking institutions because of religious discrimination. On the contrary, when the number of publications is controlled, Jews are more likely to have teaching positions in high-ranking institutions than non-Jews with the same number of publications. As was suggested in Chapter 5, Jewish scholars disproportionately start out in prestigious colleges and universities as undergraduates, and this helps to "track" them in prestigious institutions during their subsequent careers. Of course, part of the benefit of receiving early training in high-ranking institutions undoubtedly is that students develop stronger research orientations and skills that promote mobility up the academic ladder.

It could be argued that Jews are concentrated in academic disciplines that typically place greater emphasis on research or where publication occurs more frequently, and this explains their greater tendency to publish. It is true that the fields in which Jews are least concentrated, such as education and the fine arts, are generally less oriented toward research. However, even when this factor is controlled, the differences in Table 28 stand up. As an illustration, Table 29 repeats the analysis in Table 28 but does so only for social scientists. As before, Jews consistently exhibit a slightly

TABLE 29 *Research activity by religious background and institutional quality (social scientists only)*

Religious background	Universities			Colleges			Junior colleges	Total
	High	Medium	Low	High	Medium	Low		
				3 or more publications				
Protestants								
Percentage	58	45	30	24	16	8	5	24
Number	3,487	5,278	4,879	2,004	3,888	7,543	4,967	32,048
Catholics								
Percentage	57	48	32	14	9	7	6	20
Number	595	1,022	1,051	362	1,331	2,549	1,211	8,121
Jews								
Percentage	69	59	48	36	18	17	6	47
Number	1,628	910	977	640	305	422	422	5,304

higher rate of scholarly productivity, and match the productivity level of Protestants and Catholics in the next higher institutional rank.

Having established the existence of genuine religious differences in research orientation between Jews and non-Jews, the next step is to inquire into what role, if any, personal religious involvement plays in this relationship. Are persons with more traditional religious commitments less apt to have strong research orientations? And if so, does this fact help to explain differences between Jews and non-Jews with respect to research orientation and scholarly productivity?

Table 30 shows the relationship between religious commitment and the three measures of scholarship. Among all three religious groups there is a tendency for greater religiosity to be associated with lower research orientation. Once again, the figures for Catholics are virtually identical to those for Protestants. In other words, there is nothing to indicate that religiosity among Catholics is any more inimical to the scholarly ethos than religiosity among Protestants.

Among Jewish faculty the impact of religiosity is greatest on the measure of self-conception: only 24 percent of traditionalists see themselves as intellectuals, whereas 47 percent of dropouts do so. However, the difference is small with respect to scholarly activity: traditionalists are almost as likely as dropouts to publish regularly. This is consistent with the earlier finding that Jews who scored as

Scholarly orientations	Religious background		
	Protestants	Catholics	Jews
	Percentage of self-identified intellectuals		
Traditionalists	10	14	24
Modernists	17	17	36
Ethnics	17	25	34
Dropouts	28	28	47
	Percentage who prefer research		
Traditionalists	13	14	37
Modernists	18	17	35
Ethnics	30	32	44
Dropouts	37	33	51
	Percentage with 3 or more publications		
Traditionalists	15	15	41
Modernists	19	16	40
Ethnics	29	30	44
Dropouts	30	26	47

TABLE 30
Scholarly orientations by religious background and religiosity*

* The raw numbers can be found in Table 24.

traditionalists were almost as likely as less religious Jews to achieve a teaching position in a ranking university.

From a statistical point of view, the difference between Jews and non-Jews in scholarly orientation is a product of two trends: (1) more Protestants and Catholics than Jews have traditional religious commitments, and (2) among Jews religious involvement seems to be less incompatible with scholarship than is true among Protestants and Catholics.

Earlier the question was raised of whether the scholarly orientations of modernists and ethnics would more closely resemble those of traditionalists or those of dropouts. In other words, if religion tends to be incompatible with scholarship, does it require deep religious involvement before the effects become manifest or is a moderate degree of involvement sufficient? In general, the data indicate a linear progression between lower religiosity and greater scholarship. However, in the case of Protestants and Catholics, those classified as modernists more closely resemble traditionalists than either ethnics or dropouts. In other words, the fact that modernists are deeply or moderately religious is enough to produce a relatively low rate of scholarly productivity; whether or not they are conservative in their religious beliefs is of relatively little consequence. Similarly, those classified as ethnics among Protestants and Catholics resemble dropouts in their scholarly orientations. In other words, the fact that they are indifferent or opposed to religion is enough to produce a high rate of scholarly productivity; whether or not they renounce all religious ties appears to be of relatively little consequence.

Although the data point to a general incompatibility between religious involvement and scholarly orientation, one question remains. Earlier it was observed that religiosity is at lower levels in the higher-quality institutions and in the more intellectual disciplines. Does religiosity simply prevent individuals from reaching high-quality institutions, or does it continue to have an effect even among those who teach in these institutions?

Table 31 shows that religiosity has only a modest relation to

TABLE 31 *Research activity by religious background, religiosity, and institutional quality*

| Religious background | Universities | | | | | | All institutions | |
| | High | | Medium | | Low | | | |
	Percentage	Number	Percentage	Number	Percentage	Number	Percentage	Number
	3 or more publications							
Protestants								
Traditionalists	44	7,253	36	14,707	23	16,935	15	103,012
Modernists	47	7,238	36	12,166	25	12,792	19	73,303
Ethnics	57	4,428	44	5,531	28	4,760	29	22,885
Dropouts	52	8,952	46	10,449	31	7,051	30	45,563
Catholics								
Traditionalists	47	2,024	34	3,759	20	4,019	14	29,116
Modernists	38	1,723	34	3,360	24	3,480	16	25,245
Ethnics	53	467	52	806	37	652	30	3,958
Dropouts	49	1,910	43	2,132	28	1,754	26	11,397
Jews								
Traditionalists	62	1,030	48	1,344	38	657	41	5,036
Modernists	59	1,180	54	1,606	38	1,081	40	5,967
Ethnics	65	3,418	52	4,315	39	1,612	44	12,862
Dropouts	62	2,432	60	2,849	38	996	47	8,810

scholarly productivity once institutional quality is controlled. For example, among Protestants in ranking universities 44 percent of traditionalists, as compared to 52 percent of dropouts, report three or more publications in the last two years. This pattern of small differences occurs at every institutional rank for both Protestants and Catholics. (As reported earlier, religiosity generally is unrelated to scholarly productivity for Jews.) In other words, within a particular institution Protestants and Catholics with stronger religious ties are not appreciably less likely to publish regularly than their religious colleagues.

If religion impedes scholarship, its chief consequence is to channel more religious individuals into lower-ranking institutions. It appears to be of only minimal significance thereafter. Those scholars with traditional religious commitments who teach at high-quality institutions show few signs of being less productive on this account. But such individuals are less likely to reach quality institutions in the first place.

8. Religion, Politics, and Personal Values

The basic finding of the previous chapter—that faculty with strong religious commitment tend to be less productive and successful as scholars—can be challenged on the ground that this correlation does not establish a cause and effect relationship. One might concede the sheer descriptive fact that religiosity is associated with low scholarly productivity and still reject the inference that it is because of their religious orientations that these faculty are less productive. An alternative explanation might be that religious orientations are part of a much larger system of beliefs, and it is this belief system in its entirety, and not religious beliefs in particular, that is inimical to scholarship. In order to test this idea empirically, let us begin by exploring the relationship between religion and politics.[1]

RELIGION AND POLITICS

The analysis that follows proceeds in three steps. First, to what extent do Protestant, Catholic, and Jewish faculty differ in their political attitudes? Second, do political attitudes vary systematically with degree of religious involvement? And third, do differences in political orientation cancel out the effect of religiosity on scholarly productivity? This analysis attempts to isolate religious commitment from the larger matrix of related attitudes in order to assess its independent significance.

[1] For a survey of the literature on the politics of college faculty, see Lipset (1970). Lipset and Ladd have also published several papers on the politics of academia based on the Carnegie Commission surveys (Ladd & Lipset, 1971; Lipset & Ladd, 1971 & 1972). Other papers based on the Carnegie Commission surveys will be published in a forthcoming volume by Martin Trow.

Among the studies that have explored the politics of American Jews are Cohn (1958); Fuchs (1956); Glazer (1969); and Ruchames (1969). For an analysis of religion and politics among British academics, see Halsey & Trow (1971, Ch. 15).

153

Table 32 shows the responses to a long series of questions bearing on politics. The questions are divided into six categories representing a wide range of political issues that were current when the faculty survey was conducted in the spring of 1969. Whereas Table 32 reports figures for both ranking institutions and all faculty combined, it is primarily the second set of figures that is discussed in the following pages.

On almost all 27 items in Table 32 the responses of Protestant and Catholic faculty are remarkably similar. The major exception is voting behavior. In the general population Catholics have developed a traditional allegiance to the Democratic Party as a result of certain ethnic and class factors, and this pattern is reflected among faculty. Otherwise the political attitudes of Protestant and Catholic faculty are barely distinguishable from each other.

TABLE 32   *Political attitudes by religious background (ranking universities and all faculty)*

	Ranking universities			All faculty		
Political attitudes*	*Protes-tants*	*Cath-olics*	*Jews*	*Protes-tants*	*Cath-olics*	*Jews*
Conventional politics						
1. *Voted for Nixon in 1968*	30%	23%	5%	42%	25%	6%
2. *Favored Nixon at the 1968 Republican convention*	20	20	3	35	29	6
3. *Voted for Goldwater in 1964*	14	11	1	23	13	2
4. *Favored Humphrey at the 1968 Democratic convention*	43	41	36	49	46	38
Civil libertarianism						
5. *Faculty members should be free to present in class any ideas that they consider relevant. (Strongly agree)*	53	52	69	44	43	66
6. *Faculty members should be free on campus to advocate violent resistance to public authority*	27	27	44	18	20	38
7. *Undergraduates known to use marijuana regularly should be suspended or dismissed.*	36	35	19	56	53	26
8. *College officials have the right to regulate student behavior off campus. (Disagree)*	55	58	69	46	56	71
9. *With a few exceptions, the Chicago police acted reasonably in curbing the demonstrations at the Democratic National Convention.*	31	31	12	44	44	15

TABLE 32 *(continued)*

Political attitudes*	Ranking universities			All faculty		
	Protes-tants	Cath-olics	Jews	Protes-tants	Cath-olics	Jews
Student radicalism						
10. What do you think of the emergence of radical student activism in recent years? (Unreservedly approve or approve with reservations)	47	48	60	40	44	59
11. Student demonstrations have no place on a college campus. (Disagree)	42	39	54	31	32	53
12. Campus disruptions by militant students are a threat to academic freedom.	51	50	47	53	51	43
13. Students who disrupt the functioning of a college should be expelled or suspended. (Strongly agree)	44	44	35	53	51	34
14. Meaningful social change cannot be achieved through traditional American politics.	27	32	30	31	35	33
15. In the U.S.A. today there can be no justification for using violence to achieve political goals. (Strongly agree)	44	45	36	49	48	36
Black power and integration						
16. Racial integration of the public elementary schools should be achieved even if it requires busing.	55	55	67	44	47	61
17. Where de facto segregation exists, black people should be assured control over their own schools.	65	65	64	65	66	64
18. Most American colleges and universities are racist whether they mean to be or not.	39	36	42	38	36	44
19. Any institution with a substantial number of black students should offer a program of Black Studies if they wish it.	68	69	72	67	71	73
20. Any special academic program for black students should be administered and controlled by black people.	25	25	26	24	28	28
21. More minority group undergraduates should be admitted here even if it means relaxing normal academic standards of admission.	47	44	55	38	40	53
22. The normal academic requirements should be relaxed in appointing members of minority groups to the faculty here.	29	26	35	19	21	30
23. The main cause of Negro riots in the cities is white racism.	51	50	58	44	47	58

TABLE 32 *(continued)*

	Ranking universities			All faculty		
Political attitudes*	Protes-tants	Cath-olics	Jews	Protes-tants	Cath-olics	Jews
Attitudes toward the counterculture						
24. Marijuana should be legalized.	45	45	63	29	32	59
25. Hippies represent an important criticism of American culture.	54	54	60	50	55	61
International issues						
26. Which of these positions on Vietnam is closest to your own? (The U.S. should withdraw immediately or the U.S. should encourage the emergence of a coalition government.)	71	68	88	56	57	84
27. Some form of Communism is probably necessary for progress in underdeveloped countries.	19	23	27	17	20	25

*Unless otherwise indicated, percentages refer to the proportion who indicated they "strongly agree" or "agree with reservations."

In contrast to both groups, Jewish faculty are generally less likely to express politically conservative attitudes. However, the data also indicate that the greater liberalism of Jewish faculty has well-defined limits that seriously qualify the concept of "Jewish liberalism." This becomes evident by contrasting items where differences between Jews and non-Jews are greatest and those where differences are smallest.

The largest differences occur with respect to voting behavior. In the 1968 presidential election only 6 percent of all Jewish faculty voted for Nixon. In comparison, 25 percent of Catholics and 42 percent of Protestants did so. This 36 percentage point difference exceeds that produced by any of the other 26 items in Table 32.

The voting pattern in the 1964 election provides a revealing contrast. The 6 percent of Jewish faculty who voted for Nixon in 1968 is only slightly greater than the 2 percent who voted for Goldwater in 1964. In other words, by nominating a less conservative candidate in 1968, the Republican party was able to garner only an additional 4 percent of the Jewish vote. In contrast, whereas 23 percent of Protestants voted for Goldwater in 1964, 42 percent voted for Nixon in 1968 (the figures for Catholics are 13 and 25 percent). This would suggest that 23 percent of all Protestant faculty are, so to speak, as conservative as Goldwater, and another 19 percent lie along the political spectrum between Goldwater and Nixon. Gauged by their voting behavior, the greater liberalism of Jewish faculty is an indisputable fact.

Certain other issues also produce substantial differences between Jews and non-Jews. Jews were much more likely to oppose the Vietnam war, to express disapproval of the behavior of the Chicago police during the 1968 Democratic Convention, and to favor the legalization of marijuana. Jewish responses on these issues are probably best understood in terms of a traditional Jewish commitment to civil liberties, and a fear of political repression and official violence. Jews also score as more liberal on other measures of civil libertarianism. For example, they more often defend the right of faculty to present whatever ideas they wish in a classroom, and they more often oppose regulation of student behavior off campus. Civil libertarianism is one element of traditional liberalism that continues to figure prominently in Jewish political attitudes.

However, on issues associated with the political radicalism of the 1960s, differences between Jewish and non-Jewish faculty are either small or nonexistent. The different response pattern on radical issues, as compared to the traditional liberal issues, is pointed up most clearly by the eight questions concerning blacks. On the traditional issue of school integration, Jewish opinion is substantially more liberal than that of non-Jews. However, on issues connected with the black power movement, the Jewish response is not appreciably different from that of Protestants and Catholics. Thus, although Jews are a good deal more likely to support busing in order to achieve integration, they are no more likely to support the idea of black control where de facto segregation exists.

The same pattern emerges with respect to student radicalism. Although Jews are more likely than non-Jews to express approval of student activism and otherwise defend radical causes, these differences are small in comparison to those produced by questions on voting behavior. For example, 59 percent of Jewish faculty said they approved of student activism, as compared to 40 percent of Protestants and 44 percent of Catholics. This difference of 19 percentage points is small in comparison to the question on voting in the 1968 presidential election, where the difference was 36 percentage points.

On other questions, too, the data suggest that the highly charged issues of the late 1960s tested the limit of Jewish liberalism. Thus although Jews are much more likely than non-Jews to favor the legalization of marijuana, presumably on civil libertarian grounds, they are only slightly more likely to credit the hippie movement as representing an important criticism of American society. Whereas Jews disproportionately criticize the behavior of the Chicago police during the 1968 Democratic Convention, they are no more likely than non-Jews to subscribe to the view that meaningful change cannot come through traditional American politics. Nor, as we have seen, is the heavy Jewish support for black civil rights matched by an equal tendency to support the principle of black control over segregated schools. Nor are Jewish faculty much more willing than their non-Jewish colleagues to relax requirements to increase minority representation either among undergraduates or among faculty.

It would not be correct to say that Jewish faculty are in the same ideological camp as their non-Jewish colleagues, since large differences separate them on many important issues ranging from voting preference to opinion on Vietnam. However, on issues most clearly identified with the radical movement of the 1960s, opinion between Jews and non-Jews narrows considerably.

When political currents change as rapidly as they did in the 1960s, political labels are inevitably thrown into disarray. Inasmuch as Jewish intellectuals tend to identify with the Old Left, they often exhibit a discrepancy between their real attitudes and their political self-concepts, as the following analysis will demonstrate.

The proportion of faculty who perceive themselves as being left or liberal is much higher for Jews (74 percent) than for Catholics (45 percent) or Protestants (41 percent).[2] This, of course, is consistent with real differences in political orientation. But how does political self-definition vary with issues related to the New Left? To address this question an index was constructed using three items on student activism (Table 32, items 10, 11, and 13).[3] As Table 33

[2] Only 5 percent of the sample identified themselves as being "left," whereas 39 percent identified themselves as "liberal." In the analysis that follows, the combined group of "left" and "liberals" will be referred to just as "liberals."

[3] In constructing the Index of Support of Student Activism one point was given for each of the following responses: disagreeing that student demonstrations have no place on a college campus (Table 32, item 11), approving of student activism (item 10), and disagreeing that students who disrupt the functioning of a college should be expelled (item 13). The scale tends to form a Guttman pattern. Respondents with a score of 0 (conservatives) did not give any "left" responses; those with a score of 1 (moderates) generally gave a "left" response to only the first item; those with a score of 2 (liberals) gave a "left" response to the first two items; those with a score of 3 (radicals) gave a "left" response to all three items. The scale exhibits great predictive power on external items, as exemplified by its very powerful relationship to political self-identity (Table 33).

shows, Jews tend to think of themselves as liberal even when they have conservative attitudes on student activism. Among Jews who score as conservative, 39 percent still define themselves as liberals, whereas the figure for Protestants and Catholics are just 13 and 15 percent. Among those scoring as moderates, 57 percent of Jews say they are liberals, as compared to 27 percent of Protestants and 32 percent of Catholics. Only at the upper extreme of the scale — among those who actually score as radicals — is the proportion of self-defined liberals similar for both Jews and non-Jews.

The reason for this interesting discrepancy is not that Jews more often misperceive or exaggerate their political sentiments. Rather it is that Jews define their liberalism in traditional terms, such as loyalty to the Democratic Party or commitment to civil libertarian principles. Beyond these traditional issues, however, self-defined Jewish liberals are split between those who support radical trends and those who do not. Further analysis shows that this split occurs largely along age lines. Those Jewish faculty who define themselves as liberal but whose attitudes toward student activism run in a conservative direction come disproportionately from the ranks of older faculty. Hence the correlation between score on the Index of Support of Student Activism and political self-identity is highest among the youngest generation of Jewish faculty — .744. With greater age, the correlation decreases to .663, .655, and .620. The implication of this finding is that younger faculty define their political self-identities more in terms of the radical issues of the 1960s, whereas older faculty tend to define themselves in terms of older liberal issues.

TABLE 33 *Political self-definition by religious background and support of student activism*

	Religious background					
Support of student activism	Protestants		Catholics		Jews	
	Percentage	*Number*	*Percentage*	*Number*	*Percentage*	*Number*
	Defining themselves as left or liberal					
Conservatives	13	77,269	15	19,136	39	4,337
Moderates	27	92,418	32	25,009	57	10,331
Liberals	63	67,613	64	20,593	86	10,954
Radicals	87	41,711	84	12,773	95	10,647
TOTAL	41	283,273	45.	78,693	74	36,988

Now that differences in the political orientations of Protestants, Catholics, and Jews have been examined, the next step is to explore the effects of religiosity. Table 34 employs two political measures, one of a traditional kind (vote in the 1968 presidential election), the other more contemporary (attitudes toward student radicalism). In both cases religiosity is strongly related to political conservatism, and this is true of Jews as well as Protestants and Catholics. For example, among Jews the percentage scoring low on support of student activism ranges from 62 percent among traditionalists, to 43 percent among modernists, to 36 percent among ethnics, to 30 percent among dropouts. While more religious Jews were no less productive as scholars, they are clearly more conservative in their political attitudes.

Furthermore, as religious commitment goes from strong to weak, differences between Jews and non-Jews also grow smaller. Thus, among dropouts the proportion scoring low on support of student activism is 36 percent among Protestants, 33 percent among Catholics, and 30 percent among Jews. In other words, for those who renounce all religious ties there is little residual effect of religious background on political attitudes.

It is evident that religiosity and political conservatism go hand in hand among faculty just as in the population at large. This fact

TABLE 34
*Political
conservatism
by religious
background and
religiosity* *

Religiosity	Religious background		
	Protestants	*Catholics*	*Jews*
	Percentage who voted for Nixon in 1968		
Traditionalists	63	38	12
Modernists	33	18	6
Ethnics	28	22	4
Dropouts	16	11	3
TOTAL	42	25	6
	Percentage scoring low on index of support of student activism		
Traditionalists	81	78	62
Modernists	52	46	43
Ethnics	47	42	36
Dropouts	36	33	30
TOTAL	61	57	41

* The raw numbers are shown in Table 24.

raises a serious question: if religiosity is part of a larger matrix of conservative attitudes, what evidence is there that religious orientations have an independent effect on scholarship? Could the observed correlations between religiosity and low scholarly productivity be a function of a broader conservatism rather than of religious orientations per se?

Plausible as this argument may be, it receives no support in the data. Table 35 shows that there is only a small relation between political orientations and scholarly productivity. Those on the political right are only slightly less likely to publish regularly than those on the left. In contrast, we observed before that the strength of a person's religious commitments was systematically related to his research orientations and his scholarly productivity (Table 30). In other words, while religious conservatism is associated with low scholarly productivity, political conservatism is not. The significance of this finding is that it discounts the argument that the negative impact of religiosity on scholarship only reflects the operation of a larger cluster of conservative attitudes. All the evidence points to the conclusion that religious perspectives do indeed tend to be incompatible with scholarship.[4]

RELIGION AND PERSONAL VALUES To say that religion is incompatible with scholarship is not to imply that religion somehow blunts the mind. It is not altogether clear from past studies exactly what it is about religion that is the source

TABLE 35   *Frequent publication by religious background and support of student activism*

	Religious background					
Support of student activism	*Protestants*		*Catholics*		*Jews*	
	Percentage	*Number*	*Percentage*	*Number*	*Percentage*	*Number*
	3 or more publications					
Conservatives	17	76,153	16	18,704	44	4,204
Moderates	22	90,835	18	24,685	42	10,253
Liberals	24	66,563	18	20,309	46	10,837
Radicals	22	41,243	21	12,418	38	10,543
TOTAL	21	279,090	18	77,414	44	36,526

[4] Caplovitz has recently come to the same conclusion on the basis of his analysis of intellectualism and apostasy among college students (Caplovitz & Sherrow, forthcoming, Ch. 4).

of its incompatibility with scholarship. The interpretation advanced here is that religious commitment entails other related values that influence the individual's priorities in his work and his profession. As observed earlier, faculty with strong religious commitments not only publish less often, but also are less likely to think of themselves as intellectuals and more likely to emphasize teaching over research. This invites speculation that persons with strong religious commitments may not place highest priority on intellectual achievement and on research—precisely those qualities that define success and earn rewards within the academic enterprise. In other words, it may not be that more religious scholars are unable to live up to prevailing values with respect to achievement and success, but rather that they subscribe to a different set of values and priorities.

Chapter 2 contained some historical evidence supporting this interpretation. There it was observed that conservative Catholic educators have traditionally viewed science and research with skepticism. Their educational philosophy emphasized mastery of the ancient verities rather than the pursuit of specialized knowledge. In their educational program they placed more importance on the cultivation of spiritual values than on the accumulation of technical information or the development of vocational skills. This was not an educational philosophy incompatible with scholarship, but it was clearly at odds with the norms of scholarship that prevail within modern secular institutions of higher learning.

There is also evidence in the data that faculty with stronger religious convictions tend to hold values that conflict with the ones that govern contemporary higher education and its system of re-

		Religious background		
TABLE 36 *Concern for student values by religious background and religiosity*[*]	*Religiosity*	*Protestants*	*Catholics*	*Jews*
	Percentage who agree with the statement: This institution should be as concerned about students' personal values as it is with their intellectual development			
	Traditionalists	86	85	74
	Modernists	80	82	75
	Ethnics	68	69	65
	Dropouts	58	62	63
	TOTAL	77	79	70

*The raw numbers are shown in Table 24.

wards. Respondents were asked to agree or disagree with the statement: "This institution should be as concerned about students' personal values as it is with their intellectual development." As Table 36 shows, agreement directly corresponds with religious commitment: the greater the religious commitment, the higher the proportion who place as much importance on students' values as on their intellectual development. This is true in the 17 ranking universities as well as in the sample as a whole.

In addition, Table 37 shows that faculty who express concern for the personal values of students are less likely to score high on all three measures of scholarly orientation. This is true for Protes-

TABLE 37 Scholarly orientations by religious background and concern for student values		Religious background		
		Protestants	*Catholics*	*Jews*
	This institution should be as concerned about students' personal values as it is with their intellectual development.			
		Percentage of self-identified intellectuals		
	Strongly agree	14	18	34
	Agree with reservations	15	15	32
	Disagree with reservations	19	23	38
	Strongly disagree	30	29	50
		Percentage who prefer research to teaching		
	Strongly agree	13	13	30
	Agree with reservations	20	20	43
	Disagree with reservations	33	31	54
	Strongly disagree	41	36	63
		Percentage with 3 or more publications		
	Strongly agree	16	13	36
	Agree with reservations	21	19	44
	Disagree with reservations	29	25	50
	Strongly disagree	32	26	48
		Numbers		
	Strongly agree	108,891	34,069	12,117
	Agree with reservations	106,846	28,148	12,934
	Disagree with reservations	50,352	11,709	8,060
	Strongly disagree	14,884	4,457	3,678

tants, Catholics, and Jews alike. The relationship is especially strong with respect to the question that asked respondents whether they generally preferred teaching or research. Among Protestant faculty who strongly agreed that their institution should be as concerned about students' values as with their intellectual development, only 13 percent expressed a preference for research over teaching. With less emphasis on students' values, the proportion preferring research sharply increases, from 13 to 20 to 33 to 41 percent. Similar trends can be observed for Catholics and Jews.

In short, the data indicate that faculty with stronger religious convictions tend to place higher priority on the teaching functions of the university, rather than on its research activities.[5] This, in turn, is related to a belief that education should attend to the cultivation of spiritual values and not merely the cultivation of the mind. Such an outlook on the purposes and functions of the university may not be conducive to scholarly productivity or academic success. However, it is cast in a somewhat different perspective by the reaction during the 1960s against the high degree of specialization in academic disciplines, the obsession with research, and the separation of moral values from the educational process. Just as Weber ended his essay on *The Protestant Ethic and the Spirit of Capitalism* with an admonition against the dangers of uncontrolled rationalism, perhaps it is proper to acknowledge the validity of an educational philosophy that emphasizes the spiritual aspects and purposes of education. The alternative, as Weber warns, is to produce "specialists without spirit" and "sensualists without heart" (Weber, 1958, p. 182).

CONCLUSION The findings reported in Chapters 7 and 8 generally confirm the incompatibility thesis of the relation between religion and scholarship. However, to say that religion and scholarship are incompatible is not to assert a simple cause-and-effect relationship. There is no evidence that persons with strong religious commitments fail to develop scholarly orientations on this account alone. Nor can it be assumed that in a person's life history he first disavows religious

---

[5] Somewhat similar findings emerge from Earl Babbie's 1970 study of medical school faculty. Babbie found that medical faculty with stronger religious convictions were more likely to emphasize the humanistic as opposed to the scientific purposes of the medical profession (Babbie, 1970, pp. 87–97).

belief and then develops scholarly orientations; indeed, the reverse process is more plausible. However, the data do indicate that religion and scholarship tend to be incompatible, in the limited sense that they vary inversely, and that stronger degrees of one tend to be accompanied by weaker degrees of the other.

Although religiosity had little effect among Jews, Protestants and Catholics with strong religious attachments were considerably less likely to achieve a position in a ranking university. They were also less often found in the more intellectual disciplines. Still more direct evidence supporting the incompatibility thesis is that Protestant and Catholic faculty with stronger religious commitments were less likely to have scholarly orientations or to publish regularly. Finally, there was no evidence that the relationship between religiosity and low scholarly productivity is merely an artifact of the relationship between religiosity and other conventional attitudes.

While these findings point to a basic conflict between religion and scholarship, they must be balanced against certain other findings in this chapter. In the first place, the overall level of religious involvement among the nation's scholars is not nearly as low as the incompatibility thesis would suggest. In the faculty sample as a whole, 78 percent continue to have at least a nominal religious identity, 64 percent say they are deeply or moderately religious, 40 percent characterize their religious beliefs as conservative, and 25 percent attend church weekly.

Also it must be remembered that the findings supporting the incompatibility thesis, like all such findings in the social sciences, are of a probabilistic nature. Thus, although more successful and productive scholars generally are less tied to religion than their less successful colleagues, many nevertheless retain strong religious commitments. Even in the ranking universities nearly a majority of faculty say they are deeply or moderately religious. And even among social scientists in ranking universities, who are the least religious of any academic discipline, a substantial minority of about one-quarter say they are deeply or moderately religious. Thus, despite the general incompatibility between religion and scholarship, many individuals do manage to combine both perspectives.

Perhaps the most important qualification of the incompatibility thesis stems from the finding that faculty with strong religious commitments have a special view of the purposes and functions of education. They are committed to the spiritual as well as the intellectual cultivation of students, and they place greater emphasis on teaching than on research. This suggests that the incompatibility between religion and scholarship does not take the form of a crude anti-intellectualism but is grounded in values that are legitimate and valuable in academic institutions.

9. Conclusion: The Fact and Fallacy of "Jewish Intellectualism" and Catholic Anti-intellectualism"

This study has sought to assess the validity of the concept of "Jewish intellectualism" and the related concept of "Catholic anti-intellectualism." It is important to realize that these concepts do more than assume a correlation between religious background and intellectual achievement. They also imply a theory that claims to explain these differences in cultural terms. Stated simply, this theory asserts that Jews had the benefit of an intellectual tradition that placed high value on scholarship and intellectual achievement, whereas Catholics not only lacked such a tradition but actively discouraged intellectual pursuits out of a fear that faith would be undermined. It should by now be clear that there is both fact and myth in the concept of "Jewish intellectualism" and "Catholic anti-intellectualism." The findings of this study provide a basis for a more precise delineation of both concepts.

ON JEWISH INTELLECTU-ALISM

The evidence in support of the notion of Jewish intellectualism is of several kinds:

1   Jews are disproportionately represented on all levels of higher education. Even among the oldest cohort of faculty, the number of Jews far exceeds their numbers in the general population. This is consistent with the implication of the historical analysis that Jews got an early start in higher education. But the data further indicate that despite great expansion of institutions of higher learning, Jews have maintained their relative position, though recent comparisons indicate that Jewish representation is probably tapering off.

2   Jews are heavily concentrated in the highest-ranking institutions. The "invasion" of the elite undergraduate colleges during the 1920s was the beginning of a trend that would eventually produce a sizable Jewish representation at higher rungs of the academic ladder. At the present time Jews constitute 17 percent of faculty in the 17 ranking institutions.

3   Except for the professions, Jews tend to be concentrated in the more intellectual disciplines and underrepresented in the more applied fields. It
is not simply that Jews are highly represented in the social and psychological sciences, for special factors may operate to produce this pattern. Even
when Jews enter less intellectual fields, they tend to be found in branches
that involve a relatively high degree of abstract thought. Thus electrical
engineering attracts more Jews than does any other branch of engineering,
and Jewish representation is higher in physics and mathematics than in
chemistry. Jews are notable for their absence in such practical fields as
education, journalism, library science, and nursing, and in such down-
to-earth fields as zoology, biology, botany, and geology.

4   In comparison to Protestants and Catholics, Jewish faculty are more apt
to see themselves as intellectual, to prefer research over teaching, and to
publish regularly. Even controlling for the effects of institutional quality
and academic discipline, Jews exhibit a higher rate of scholarly productivity.

5   There is no indication that scholarly orientations among Jews are directly
a product of a religious ethos. At least it is not the case that more religious
Jews are more likely to score high on measures of scholarly orientation.
But neither are they less likely to have scholarly orientations. In contrast
to patterns among Protestants and Catholics, religious involvement for
Jews does not appear to be incompatible with scholarship, and in this
limited sense there may be a distinctive religious element in Jewish intellectualism.

These five findings constitue the fact of "Jewish intellectualism."
However, they must be balanced against other findings that, at
the least, define the outer limits of Jewish intellectualism. Three
such findings may be singled out:

1   Although Jews have been prominent in the ranks of writers, artists, and
musicians, they are not highly represented in the academic branches of
these fields. Even among young faculty, Jewish representation in the humanities and fine arts is no higher than in engineering. Insofar as these
fields represent a unique intellectual tradition, one must conclude that it
is a tradition in which Jews have participated to a rather small degree.

2   A second qualification on "Jewish intellectualism" concerns structural
properties of higher education that historically benefited Jews. It was by
historical accident that the tide of Jewish immigration from Eastern Europe
coincided with the emergence of the modern university. Not only did enrollments grow rapidly, but the purposes of education were redefined.
Technical and vocational training became accepted as legitimate activities
for a college, and this led to the growth of professional schools which were
compatible with Jewish inclinations. Social science, another heavily Jewish

field, was also becoming established in American higher education. In short, Jews entered a situation of expanding opportunities and to some extent were carried along by the momentum of educational change.

3   A third qualification of the notion of Jewish intellectualism concerns characteristics of Jews themselves. As Chapter 4 showed in detail, certain attributes of Jewish immigrants placed them in a favorable position in comparison to most other immigrant groups. The fact that Russian Jews had previous industrial skills and experience in commerce accelerated their economic mobility, and like every middle-class group, Jews had the inclination and the economic resources to send their children to college. Even more pertinent to the question of educational attainment is the fact that Jewish immigrants had a comparatively high rate of literacy. Even if the Jewish intellectual tradition consisted of nothing else, this factor alone would have produced a higher level of educational attainment than was achieved by other immigrant groups.

The problem with cultural theories that explain Jewish success in terms of Jewish values is not that they are incorrect, but rather that they are superficial. They are correct in the sense that Jews did have the benefit of a rich intellectual tradition and did place unusually high value on education and intellectual achievement. But cultural theories are trivial unless they go on to examine the broad structural factors that buttressed this value system as well as the favorable structure of opportunity that permitted values to become realities.

ON CATHOLIC ANTI-INTELLECTU-ALISM   Much of what has been said about the fact and fallacy of "Jewish intellectualism" applies in reverse to Catholics. As was seen in Chapter 2, American Catholics had great difficulty in adjusting certain of their core values to the requirements of modern secular education. This value conflict had both religious and ethnic sources, and was a major factor in explaining why Catholicism, in Richard Hofstadter's words, "has failed to develop an intellectual tradition in America or to produce its own class of intellectuals. . ." (Hofstadter, 1962, p. 136). However, this harsh assessment is offset by several findings of this study.

The most important among these is the finding that there is a substantial uptrend in Catholic representation in the nation's colleges and universities. Although Catholics continue to be underrepresented among faculty, age breakdowns indicate that their numbers have been gradually increasing over several decades. This is true of the ranking universities as well as institutions of lower quality. In addition, Catholics presently constitute 25 percent of all graduate students (precisely their proportion in the national population), and they constitute 29 percent of all undergraduates (27 percent of those in ranking universities). It is evident that Catholics are belatedly taking their place in American higher education.

Furthermore, throughout this study Catholics have been found to resemble Protestants in their attitudes and professional orientations. In terms of religion, science, and politics, Protestant and Catholic scholars were far more notable for their similarity than for their differences. Furthermore, although religious involvement among Catholics showed signs of incompatibility with scholarship, this was no more the case than among Protestants. In short, the evidence does not support claims of a special anti-intellectualism among Catholics.

Given the handicaps with which Catholic immigrants started life in America, it is not surprising that they required another generation or two to produce their numerical share of scholars and scientists. Thomas O'Dea (1958, p. 93) is simply wrong when he writes that we "cannot attribute to immigration and problems of assimilation the absence of intellectual life" among Catholics. The fact that the great majority of Catholic immigrants came from peasant backgrounds was of enormous consequence. Not only did high levels of illiteracy slow the pace of cultural adjustment, but Catholic immigrants also lacked the kinds of occupational skills that facilitated economic mobility for Jews. These conditions also presented formidable obstacles to intellectual achievement. However, as Catholics have gradually improved their position in the class system, their children are increasingly going to college, and, as in every group, a certain number of them follow academic careers and become scholars of distinction. The scenario is the same as for other groups. It has only taken longer to play itself out.

References

"The American Jew Today," *Newsweek,* vol. 77, p. 63, March 1, 1971.

Anderson, Elin L.: *We Americans,* Harvard University Press, Cambridge, Mass., 1937.

Aries, Philippe: *Centuries of Childhood: A Social History of Family Life,* Alfred A. Knopf, Inc., New York, 1962.

Babbie, Earl R.: *Science and Morality in Medicine,* University of California Press, Berkeley, 1970.

Baker, George E. (ed.): *The Life of William E. Seward,* J. D. Redfield, New York, 1955.

Barry, Colman J.: *The Catholic Church and German Americans,* The Catholic University of America Press, Washington, D. C., 1953.

Billington, Ray Allen: *The Protestant Crusade,* Quadrangle Books, Inc., Chicago, 1964.

Boese, Thomas: *Public Education in the City of New York,* Harper & Row, Publishers, Incorporated, New York, 1869.

Bourne, William Oland: *History of the Public School Society,* William Wood & Company, New York, 1870.

Broun, Heywood, and George Britt: *Christians Only,* Vanguard Press, Inc., New York, 1931.

Brownson's Quarterly Review, vol. 2, July 1857, in Frank L. Christ and Gerald E. Sherry (eds.), *American Catholicism and the Intellectual Ideal,* Appleton-Century-Crofts, New York, 1961.

Bull, George: "The Function of the Catholic Graduate School," 1938, pp. 112–115 in Frank L. Christ and Gerald E. Sherry (eds.), *American Catholicism and the Intellectual Ideal,* Appleton-Century-Crofts, Inc., New York, 1961.

Burns, James A.: *The Catholic School System in the United States,* Benziger Bros., Inc., New York, 1908.

Cahan, Abraham: *The Rise of David Levinsky,* Colophon Books, New York, 1960.

Caplovitz, David, and Fred Sherrow: *The Religious Dropouts: A Study of Apostates Among College Graduates,* forthcoming.

"The Child: Citizen of Two Worlds," 1950, reprinted in Neil G. McCluskey, *Catholic Education in America,* Columbia University Bureau of Publications, New York, 1964.

"The Children of Immigrants in Schools," *Reports of the Immigration Commission,* vol. 1, U.S. Government Printing Office, Washington, D.C., 1911.

Christ, Frank L., and Gerald E. Sherry (eds.): *American Catholicism and the Intellectual Ideal,* Appleton-Century-Crofts, New York, 1961.

Cohn, Werner: "The Politics of American Jews," in Marshall Sklare (ed.), *The Jews,* The Free Press, New York, 1958.

Comte, Auguste: *Introduction to Positive Philosophy,* The Bobbs-Merrill Company, Inc., Indianapolis, 1970.

Conway, James: "Catholic Education in the United States," address prepared for the Catholic Congress at Melbourne, Australia, and published in *The Catholic Mind,* vol. 2, 1904.

Cook, William W.: *American Institutions and Their Preservation,* Norwood Press, Norwood, Mass., 1927.

Counts, George Sylvester: "The Selective Character of American Secondary Education," *Supplementary Educational Monographs,* no. 19, The University of Chicago Press, Chicago, 1922.

Covello, Leonard: *The Social Background of the Italo-American School Child,* edited with an introduction by Francesco Cordasco, E. J. Brill, N. B., Leiden, Netherlands, 1967, and Rowman and Littlefield, Publishers, Totowa, N.J., 1972.

Cowen, Philip: *Prejudice Against the Jew,* Philip Cowen, New York, 1928.

Cremin, Lawrence, A.: *The Transformation of the School,* Alfred A. Knopf, Inc., New York, 1961.

Cross, Robert D.: *The Emergence of Liberal Catholicism in America,* Quadrangle Books, Inc, Chicago, 1968.

Duncan, Beverly, and Otis Dudley Duncan: "Minorities and the Process of Stratification," *American Sociological Review,* vol. 33, pp. 356–364, June 1968.

Durkheim, Emile: *Suicide,* The Free Press, Glencoe, Ill., 1958.

Earnest, Ernest: *Academic Procession,* The Bobbs-Merrill Company, Inc., Indianapolis, 1953.

Ellis, John T.: *Documents of American Catholic History,* The Bruce Publishing Company, Milwaukee, 1956.

Engleman, Uriah: "The Jewish Synagogue in America," *American Journal of Sociology,* vol. 41, pp. 44–51, July 1921.

Ernst, Robert: *Immigrant Life In New York City, 1825–1863,* Ira J. Friedman, Inc., Port Washington, N.Y., 1965.

"Exclusion from College," *The Outlook,* vol. 131, pp. 406–407, July 5, 1922.

Feldman, Saul: *Escape from the Doll's House: Women in Graduate and Professional School Education,* McGraw-Hill Book Company, New York, 1974.

Feuer, Lewis S.: *The Scientific Intellectual,* Basic Books, Inc., Publishers, New York, 1963.

Francis, Alexander: *Americans,* Andrew Melrose, London, 1909.

Freud, Sigmund: *Future of an Illusion,* Schocken, New York, 1962.

Fuchs, Lawrence H.: *The Political Behavior of American Jews,* The Free Press, New York, 1956.

Gabel, Richard J.: *Public Funds for Church and Private Schools,* The Catholic University of America Press, Washington, 1937.

Gannett, Lewis S.: "Is America Anti-Semitic?" *The Nation,* vol. 115, pp. 330–332, March 14, 1923.

Gans, Herbert: *The Urban Villagers,* The Free Press, New York, 1962.

Glazer, Nathan: "Social Characteristics of American Jews, 1654–1954," *American Jewish Yearbook,* vol. 56, pp. 3–41, The American Jewish Committee and The Jewish Publication Society of America, Philadelphia, 1955.

Glazer, Nathan: *American Judaism,* The University of Chicago Press, Chicago, 1957.

Glazer, Nathan: "The New Left and the Jews," *Jewish Journal of Sociology,* vol. 11, pp. 121–132, December 1969.

Glazer, Nathan, and Daniel Moynihan: *Beyond the Melting Pot,* The M.I.T. Press, Cambridge, Mass., 1963.

Gleason, Philip: "Immigration and American Intellectual LIfe," *The Review of Politics,* vol. 26, pp. 147–173, 1964.

Glenn, Norval D., and Ruth Hyland: "Religious Preference and Worldly Success," *American Sociological Review,* vol. 32, pp. 73–85, February 1967.

Glock, Charles Y., and Rodney Stark: *Religion and Science in Tension,* Rand McNally & Company, Chicago, 1965.

Goldstein, Sidney: "Socioeconomic Differentials among Religious Groups in the United States," *American Journal of Sociology,* vol. 74, p. 612, May 1969.

Gourman, Jack: *The Gourman Report,* The Continuing Education Institute, Phoenix, 1967.

Greeley, Andrew M.: "Anti-Intellectualism in Catholic Colleges," *American Catholic Sociological Review,* vol. 23, pp. 350–368, Spring 1962.

Greeley, Andrew M.: *Religion and Career,* Sheed & Ward, Inc., New York, 1963.

Greeley, Andrew M.: *Why Can't They Be Like Us?,* E. P. Dutton & Co., Inc., New York, 1971.

Greeley, Andrew M., and Peter H. Rossi: *The Education of Catholic Americans,* Aldine Publishing Company, Chicago, 1966.

Haag, Ernest van den: *The Jewish Mystique,* Stein and Day Incorporated New York, 1969.

Halsey, A. H., and M. A. Trow: *The British Academics,* Harvard University Press, Cambridge, Mass., 1971.

Ham, William T.: "Harvard Student Opinion on the Jewish Question," *The Nation,* vol. 115, pp. 225–227, Sept. 6, 1922.

Handlin, Oscar: "How U.S. Anti-Semitism Really Began," *Commentary, The Nation,* vol. 11, p. 541, June 1951.

Handlin, Oscar: *Race and Nationality in American Life,* Doubleday and Company, Inc., Garden City, N.Y., 1957.

Handlin, Oscar: *Boston's Immigrants,* Atheneum Publishers, New York, 1968.

Handlin, Oscar, and Mary F. Handlin: "The Acquisition of Political and Social Rights by the Jews in the United States," *American Jewish Yearbook,* vol. 56, American Jewish Committee, New York, 1955.

Hapgood, Norman: "Jews and College Life," *Harper's Weekly,* vol. 62, p. 54, 1916a.

Hapgood, Norman: "Schools, Colleges and Jews," *Harper's Weekly,* vol. 62, p. 78, Jan. 22, 1916b.

"Harvard 'Talk' about Jews," *Literary Digest,* vol. 73, p. 28, June 24, 1922.

Heath, Solyman: *Reports of Cases in Law and Equity Determined by the Supreme Judicial Court of Maine,* vol. 38, Masters, Smith, & Co., Hallowell, 1856.

Higham John: "Social Discrimination Against Jews in America, 1830–1930," *Publication of the American Jewish Historical Society,* Waltham, Mass., vol. 47, no. 1, September 1957.

Hofstadter, Richard: *Anti-Intellectualism in American Life,* Vintage Books, Random House, Inc., New York, 1963.

Huntington, Ellsworth, and Leon F. Whitney: "Religion and 'Who's Who,'" *American Mercury,* vol. 2, no. 44, pp. 438–443, August 1927.

"Instruction of the Congregation of Propaganda de Fide," 1875, in John T. Ellis (ed.), *Documents of American Catholic History,* The Bruce Publishing Company, Milwaukee, 1956.

Jenks, Jeremiah W., and W. Jett Lauck: *The Immigration Problem,* Funk & Wagnalls, a division of Reader's Digest Books, Inc., New York, 1912.

"The Jews and the Colleges," *World's Work,* vol. 44, p. 352, 1922.

Kallen, Horace M.: "The Roots of Anti-Semitism," *The Nation,* vol. 116, pp. 240–242, Feb. 28, 1923.

Kaplan, Abraham: *The Conduct of Inquiry,* Chandler Publishing Company, San Francisco, 1964.

Keppel, Frederich Paul: *Columbia,* Oxford University Press, New York, 1914.

Knapp, Robert H., and H. B. Goodrich: *Origins of American Scientists,* The University of Chicago Press, Chicago, 1952.

Knapp, Robert H., and J. J. Greenbaum: *The Younger American Scholar: His Collegiate Origins,* The University of Chicago Press, Chicago, 1953.

Kohn, Melvin L., and Carmi Schooler: "Class, Occupation, and Orientation," *American Sociological Review,* vol. 34, pp. 659–677, October 1969.

Kramer, Judith: *The American Minority Community,* Thomas Y. Crowell Company, New York, 1970.

Kramer, Victor A.: "What Lowell Said," *The American Hebrew,* p. 391ff., Jan. 26, 1923.

Ladd, Everett, Jr., and Seymour Martin Lipset: "The Politics of American Political Scientists," *Political Science,* vol. 4, pp. 135–144, Spring 1971.

Lannie, Vincent P.: *Public Money and Parochial Education,* The Press of Case Western Reserve University, Cleveland, 1968.

Lehman, Harvey C., and Paul A. Witty: "Scientific Eminence and Church Membership," *Scientific Monthly,* vol. 33, pp. 544–549, December 1931.

Levine, Edward M.: *Irish and Irish Politicians,* University of Notre Dame Press, Notre Dame, Ind., 1966.

Levitan, Tina: *The Laureates: Jewish Winners of the Nobel Prize,* Twayne Publishers, Inc., New York, 1960.

Lewis, Oscar: *La Vida,* Vintage Books, Random House, Inc., New York, 1968.

Lipset, Seymour Martin: "The Politics of Academia," in David C. Nichols (ed.), *Perspectives on Campus Tensions,* American Council on Education, Washington, D.C., 1970.

Lipset, Seymour Martin, and Everett Ladd, Jr.: "Jewish Academics in the United States: Their Achievements, Culture, and Politics," *American Jewish Yearbook,* vol. 72, American Jewish Committee, New York, 1971.

Lipset, Seymour Martin, and Everett Ladd, Jr.: "The Politics of American Sociologists," *American Journal of Sociology,* vol. 78, pp. 67–104, July 1972.

Mack, Raymond, Raymond Murphy, and Seymour Yellin: "The Protestant Ethic, Level of Aspiration, and Social Mobility: An Empirical Test," *American Sociological Review,* vol. 21, pp. 295–300, June 1956.

"May Jews Go to College?" *The Nation,* vol. 114, p. 708, 1922.

McCluskey, Neil G. (ed.): *Catholic Education in America,* Columbia University Bureau of Publications, New York, 1964.

McCluskey, Neil G.: "A Changing Pattern," in Daniel Callahan (ed.), *Federal Aid and Catholic Schools,* Helicon Press, Inc., Baltimore, 1964.

McGuire, Martin R. P.: "The Function of the University in American Life," 1939, in Frank L. Christ and Gerard E. Sherry (eds.), *American Catholicism and the Intellectual Ideal,* Appleton-Century-Crofts, Inc., New York, 1961.

Merton, Robert: "Puritanism, Pietism, and Science," in *Social Theory and Social Structure,* The Free Press, Glencoe, Ill., 1963.

Meyer, R. H.: "The Catholic Chaplain at the Secular University," *Catholic Educational Association Bulletin,* vol. 4, no. 1, pp. 150–180, November 1907.

Miller, Herbert Adolfus: *The School and the Immigrants,* Wm. F. Fall, Cleveland, 1916.

Monroe, Paul: *Founding of the American Public School System,* The Macmillan Company, New York, 1940.

Morison, Samuel Eliot: *Three Centuries of Harvard,* Harvard University Press, Cambridge, Mass., 1936.

Myers, Gustavus: *History of Bigotry in the United States,* Capricorn Books, G. P. Putnam's Sons, New York, 1960.

Nelli, Humbert S.: *The Italians in Chicago 1880–1930,* Oxford Book Company, Inc., New York, 1970.

New York Times, June 2, 1922; June 4, 1922; June 6, 1922; June 7, 1922; June 17, 1922; June 23, 1922; January 12, 1923; January 16, 1923; January 23, 1923.

O'Dea, Thomas: *American Catholic Dilemma,* Sheed & Ward, Inc., New York, 1958.

Palmer, A. Emerson: *The New York Public School,* The Macmillan Company, New York, 1905.

"Pastoral Letter of 1852," The First Plenary Council of Baltimore, in Neil G. McCluskey (ed.), *Catholic Education in America,* Columbia University Bureau of Publications, New York, 1964.

"Pastoral Letter of 1866," The Second Plenary Council of Baltimore, in Neil G. McCluskey (ed.)., *Catholic Education in America,* Columbia University Bureau of Publications, New York, 1964.

"Pastoral Letter of 1884," The Third Plenary Council of Baltimore, in Neil G. McCluskey (ed.), *Catholic Education in America,* Columbia University Bureau of Publications, New York, 1964.

"Pastoral Letter of the Provincial Council of Baltimore," 1829, in Neil G. McCluskey (ed.), *Catholic Education in America,* Columbia University Bureau of Publications, New York, 1964.

"Pastoral Letter of the Provincial Council of Baltimore," 1840, in Neil G. McCluskey (ed.), *Catholic Education in America,* Columbia University Bureau of Publications, New York, 1964.

Podhoretz, Norman: *Making It,* Random House, Inc., New York, 1967.

Report of the Committee Appointed "To Consider and Report to the Governing Boards Principles and Methods for More Effective Selecting of Candidates for Admission to the University," Harvard University, Cambridge, Mass., April 1923.

Reports of the Immigration Commission, 41 vols., U.S. Government Printing Office, Washington, D.C., 1911; reprinted by Arno Press, New York, 1970.

Reports of the Industrial Commission on Immigration, vol. 15, U.S. Government Printing Office, Washington, D.C., 1901.

Rhodes, A. Lewis, and Charles B. Nam: "The Religious Context of Educational Expectations," *American Sociological Review,* vol. 35, pp. 253–267, April 1970.

Riis, Jacob: *How the Other Half Lives,* Hill and Wang, Inc., New York, 1957.

Rischin, Moses: *The Promised City: New York Jews, 1870–1914,* Harvard University Press, Cambridge, Mass., 1962.

Rosen, Bernard: "Race, Ethnicity, and the Achievement Syndrome," *American Sociological Review,* vol. 24, pp. 47–60, February 1959.

Rubinow, Israel: "The Economic Condition of Jews in Russia," *Bulletin of the Bureau of Labor,* no. 72, pp. 487–583, U.S. Government Printing Office, Washington, D.C., 1907.

Ruchames, Louis: "Jewish Radicalism in the United States," in Peter I. Rose (ed.), *The Ghetto and Beyond,* Random House, Inc., New York, 1969.

Rudolph, Frederick: *The American College and University,* Random House, Inc., New York, 1962.

Rudy, S. Willis: *The College of the City of New York: A History, 1847–1947,* The City College Press, New York, 1949.

Russell, Francis: "The Coming of the Jews," *The Antioch Review,* vol. 15, pp. 19–38, March 1955.

Sanders, Ronald: *Downtown Jews,* Harper & Row, Publishers, Incorporated, New York, 1969.

Selznick, Gertrude, and Stephen Steinberg: *The Tenacity of Prejudice,* Harper & Row, Publishers, Incorporated, New York, 1969.

Siu, Paul: "The Sojourner," *American Journal of Sociology,* vol. 8, pp. 34–44, July 1952.

Slater, Miriam K.: "My Son the Doctor: Aspects of Mobility among American Jews," *American Sociological Review,* vol. 34, no. 3, pp. 359–373, June 1969.

Stark, Rodney, and Charles Y. Glock: *American Piety: The Nature of Religious Commitment,* University of California Press, Berkeley, 1968.

Steinberg Stephen: "Reform Judaism: The Origin and Evolution of a 'Church Movement,'" *Journal for the Scientific Study of Religion,* vol. 5, pp. 117–129, Fall 1965.

Stephenson, George M.: *A History of American Immigration, 1820–1924,* Ginn and Company, Boston, 1926.

Strodtbeck, Fred L.: "Family Interaction, Values, and Achievement," in David C. McClelland, Alfred L. Baldwin, Urie Bronfenbrenner, and Fred L. Strodtbeck (eds.), *Talent and Society,* D. Van Nostrand Company, Inc., Princeton, N.J., 1958.

Thomas, W. I., and Florian Znaniecki: *The Polish Peasant in Europe and America,* Alfred A. Knopf, Inc., New York, 1927.

Trow, Martin, et. al.: *Technical Report: National Surveys of Higher Education,* Survey Research Center, University of California, Berkeley, 1971.

Trow, Martin: *Essays on American Higher Education (working title),* McGraw Hill Book Company, New York, forthcoming.

U.S. Bureau of the Census: *Current Population Reports,* series p. 20, no. 79, February 2, 1958.

Veblen, Thorstein: "The Intellectual Pre-eminence of Jews in Modern Europe," in Max Lerner (ed.), *The Portable Veblen,* The Viking Press, Inc., New York, 1948.

Veblen, Thorstein: *The Higher Learning in America,* Sagamore Press, New York, 1967.

Veroff, Joseph, and Sheila Feld: "Achievement Motivation and Religious Background," *American Sociological Review,* vol. 27, pp. 205–217, 1962.

Veysey, Lawrence R.: *The Emergence of the American University,* The University of Chicago Press, Chicago, 1965.

Ware, Caroline: *Greenwich Village, 1920–1930,* Colophon Books, Harper & Row Publishers, Incorporated, New York, 1965.

Warren, Bruce L.: "Socioeconomic Achievement and Religion, the American Case," *Sociological Inquiry,* vol. 40, pp. 130–155, Spring 1970.

Weber, Max: *The Protestant Ethic and the Spirit of Capitalism,* Charles Scribner's Sons, New York, 1958.

Weyl, Nathaniel: *The Creative Elite in America,* Public Affairs Press, Washington, D.C., 1966.

Weyl, Nathaniel, and Stefan Possony; *The Geography of Intellect,* Henry Regnery Company, Chicago, 1963.

White, Morton: "Reflections on Anti-Intellectualism," *Daedalus,* vol. 91, pp. 457–468, Summer 1962.

"Why a Jewish University?" in Louis I. Newman, *A Jewish University in America?,* Bloch Publishing Company, New York, 1923.

Wiener, Norbert: *Ex Prodigy,* The M.I.T. Press, Cambridge, Mass. 1966.

Williams, Phyllis H.: *South Italian Folkways in Europe and America,* Yale University Press, New Haven, Conn., 1938.

Zborowski, Mark: "The Place of Book-Learning in Traditional Jewish Culture," in Margaret Mead and Martha Wolfenstein (eds.), *Childhood in Contemporary Cultures,* The University of Chicago Press, Chicago, 1955.

Zborowski, Mark, and Elizabeth Herzog: *Life Is with People: The Culture of the Shtetl,* Schocken Books, Inc., New York, 1962. Originally published by International Universities Press, Inc., New York, 1952.

Zelan, Joseph: "Religious Apostasy, Higher Education and Occupational Choice," *Sociology of Education,* vol. 41, no. 4, pp. 370–379, Fall 1968.

Index

This book was set in Vladimir by University Graphics, Inc.
It was printed on acid-free, long-life paper and bound by The
Maple Press Company. The designers were Elliot Epstein and
Edward Butler. The editors were Nancy Tressel and Janine Parson
for McGraw-Hill Book Company and Verne A. Stadtman and Sidney
J. P. Hollister for the Carnegie Commission on Higher Education.
Bill Greenwood and Milton Heiberg supervised the production.